May 1889:
The French architect Lucien Fournerea
returns from a stay in Angkor and
hibits seven large drawings of the temp
Angkor Wat at the Paris Salon, followi
m in 1890 with seven large-scale drawi
the Baphuon. They were not seen aga
l October 1989. A selection is reprodu
above and on the following pages

ANNAM

B G E

COCHINCHINE

FRANÇAISE

MER DE CHINE

Relevé et dessiné par l'architecte sou
PARIS _ Mars 1883.

ÉTAT

COUPE LONGITU

EST OUEST

CONTENTS

ANGKOR
HEART OF AN ASIAN EMPIRE

Bruno Dagens

DISCOVERIES

HARRY N. ABRAMS, INC., PUBLISHERS

"Here then are those temples which for so long seemed like visions…. Here are the foundations, the plinths, the galleries, the extraordinary domes resembling multi-ringed tiaras. All that is missing is the tropical forest sprawling under the Asian sky, from which torrents pour one moment, bringing floods but not relief, giving way the next moment to a pitiless sun, which beats down, bringing sunstroke and death."

Claude Farrère, *L'Illustration*, 1931

CHAPTER I

DISCOVERY? IS THAT THE WORD?

Opposite: Angkor Wat as it was shown at the Colonial Exposition in Paris (1931). Right: Detail of a sculpture on the southern causeway of Angkor Thom.

A Killjoy Missionary

By 1874 Henri Mouhot's posthumous glory was firmly established. Articles and books hailed him as the "discoverer" of the former capital of Cambodia. The magnificent official publication devoted to Ernest Doudart de Lagrée and Francis Garnier's voyage of exploration had just appeared, supplementing the brief descriptions by Mouhot and his early successors. There was one person, however, who was not happy about all this: a French missionary, Father Charles-Emile Bouillevaux, who regarded these "discoveries" as "charlatanism." Angkor had not been "discovered," he said, for the good reason that it had never been lost or forgotten in the first place. He himself had visited it and published a short account of his visit before Mouhot had even left Europe. What was more, he was by no means the first: Angkor had already been mentioned by various missionaries, by Portuguese travelers in the 16th century, and even by a few Chinese chroniclers in the 13th. While the recent publications certainly were interesting, "Let us not exaggerate," he said.

Father Bouillevaux was right in fact, even if he was out of sympathy with the spirit of the times: Europe was keen to "discover" the world and would not readily be denied. Besides, Mouhot had never claimed to have discovered anything and even quoted Bouillevaux in his own account. Doudart de Lagrée and Garnier also knew of the missionaries and Portuguese explorers and were familiar, in particular, with the work of Chou Ta-kuan, the Chinese emissary who at the end of the 13th century spent almost a year in what was then the capital of Cambodia.

A Chinese Among "Barbarians"

In 1296 Chou Ta-kuan, like Marco Polo a few years earlier, sailed along the coast of what is now Vietnam. Instead of continuing toward Indonesia, however, he headed inland up the Mekong River,

Henri Mouhot's *Voyage à Siam et dans le Cambodge* (Expedition to Siam and Cambodia, 1868) brought Angkor to public attention.

Chou Ta-kuan's contemporary, Marco Polo (center, flanked by Chinese dignitaries), had left Beijing in 1291 to sail back to Venice.

leaving it to enter the Tonle Sap, the Great Lake that lies in the heart of the Cambodian plain. Crossing the lake, he disembarked on its northeastern bank, not far from Angkor. Chou Ta-kuan, who was accompanying a mission to extract homage for his master, the Chinese emperor, arrived at the Cambodian capital in August 1296 and remained there until July 1297.

There was nothing particularly extraordinary about such a journey. The Chinese had long entertained diplomatic and commercial relations with Chenla, as they called Cambodia. This was not the first such mission and would not be the last. Moreover, there was a thriving Chinese community in Angkor composed of merchants and sailors who had jumped ship, many of whom had been established there for quite some time.

The sumptuousness of the Chinese court (above) reinforced the sense of superiority the Chinese felt toward those peoples they regarded as Barbarians. Though sparing in his praise, Chou Ta-kuan nevertheless wrote a precise, detailed, and personal account that brings to life the city of Angkor Thom, capital of one of the most powerful states of Southeast Asia.

A Whirlwind Guide for Tourists

What made Chou Ta-kuan's visit to Cambodia so significant was the account of it he gave on his return. In his *Memorials on the Customs of Cambodia* he sketches in

At Angkor in 1296–7 Chou Ta-kuan witnessed the king granting audiences from his "golden window." A similar custom still prevailed in Thailand four hundred years later. This engraving (left) shows the king, Phra Narai, receiving Louis XIV's emissary, the Chevalier de Chaumont, on 18 October 1685. Two years later it was the turn of another French ambassador, Simon de La Loubère.

> **"**[The king] merely makes an appearance at a window, in the manner formerly adopted by the king of China. The window belongs to an upper chamber, at what appears to be second-floor level, overlooking the reception room. It measures about nine feet in height and three steps had to be erected beneath it so that I could reach up and place the king's letter directly in the hands of the king of Siam.**"**
>
> Simon de La Loubère
> *Du Royaume de Siam*
> (Of the Kingdom of Siam)
> 1691

the scene for his report by describing the capital, the "Walled City," and its immediate vicinity. Chou Ta-kuan describes the permanent structures—the walls and city temples and a few neighboring temples—and then shifts his attention to the royal dwellings and the homes of the city's other inhabitants, buildings constructed in less-durable materials. What we end up with is a brief guide to the most important sites in the capital and a handful of places of interest in the vicinity.

The "Walled City"

The "Walled City" was the huge rectangular complex with a surrounding wall and a vast moat known to the Cambodians as Angkor Thom (meaning "Angkor-the-Great" or "Great City"). The wall with its five gateways particularly impressed Chou Ta-kuan, as it was to impress Portuguese travelers in the 16th century. He has less to say, on the other hand, about the huge temple-mountains, although he was clearly struck by their complexity, the gilding or metal cladding of their superstructures, and the gold statues, concluding: "I imagine it is these monuments that account for the glowing reports foreign merchants have always given of rich and noble Cambodia."

Of the royal palace he saw only the public areas, during audiences when the king appeared at his "golden window." Chou Ta-kuan nevertheless gathered that "the palace housed numerous marvels" and was able to state that "the long verandas and covered corridors stretch out and interconnect in a not inharmonious way." In front of the palace, beyond the great esplanade, he noted "twelve small stone towers"—today known as the Towers of the Rope Dancers—whose purpose, according to Chou Ta-kuan, was bound up with divine judgments.

Outside the city he mentions just a few significant

Jayavarman VII (1180–1218?) was the last great king of Angkor. His death coincided with a decline in his country's fortunes. Its resources were exhausted by his ambitious building schemes, and its political power was eroded by internal conflicts and a series of wars with Thailand.

landmarks, including the "tomb of Lu Pan," which is none other than the temple of Angkor Wat. Two temples built in the middle of huge artificial lakes also excited his interest, and he describes the one in the "Eastern Lake" (a temple now known as the Eastern Mebon) as housing "a recumbent bronze Buddha from whose navel a constant stream of water flows."

What Chou Ta-kuan took for a marvelous Buddha was this 11th-century bronze sculpture of Vishnu, discovered in 1938. Though he claimed it was in the "Eastern Lake," it was found in the Mebon, or island temple, in the Western Baray.

The King, His Court, and the People

The king was regarded as a being endowed with magical, protective powers. It was said that for the good of his kingdom he made love each night to a spirit, a nine-headed serpent who appeared in the guise of a woman.

On the rare occasions when he left the palace, the king, carrying a golden sword, would travel mounted on an elephant and accompanied by a horde of attendants. The respect in which he was held showed, according to Chou Ta-kuan, that "although they are Barbarians, these people nevertheless know what a prince is."

Like all other women, the royal wives, of whom there were five—one for the chief apartment and one for each of the cardinal points—went about barefoot, wore their hair in chignons, and left their breasts, described by Chou Ta-kuan as "white as milk," uncovered. Such whiteness resulted from the fact that they were never exposed to the sun, the Cambodians being as a general rule "very black."

Dignitaries and court officials traveled the streets in palanquins with golden shafts, accompanied, depending

A royal audience, one of the many reliefs in the Bayon depicting scenes from the life of the monarch.

"Only the prince may wear cloth patterned all over with leaves. He wears a golden diadem. … Instead of the diadem sometimes he simply winds around his head a garland of scented flowers not unlike jasmine. Around his neck he wears about three pounds of large pearls and around his wrists, ankles, and arms gold bracelets and rings."

Chou Ta-kuan

on their rank, by a greater or lesser number of attendants carrying gold parasols. Members of various religious sects were much in evidence—educated Brahmans attached to the court, Buddhist monks in their yellow robes, and followers of Shiva. As for the common folk, according to Chou Ta-kuan they were extremely simple, and at the sight of a Chinese man they prostrated themselves on the ground.

He notes a number of different festivals, including one celebrating the first month of the new year and another involving the ritual bathing of statues of the Buddha. Foreign dignitaries were invited to the most important festivals, which took place on the great esplanade in front of the palace, attended by crowds of worshipers.

Was the City Abandoned?

Almost a century and a half after Chou Ta-kuan's visit—in around 1431—the king of Cambodia left Angkor Thom, and the court moved south, beyond the Great Lake

Chou Ta-kuan was struck by the graceful simplicity of the Cambodian people. Despite their elaborate headdresses, these *devatas*, or divinities, on a relief at Angkor Wat display the same quality.

One of Jayavarman VII's wives may have served as the model for this sandstone sculpture of Infinite Wisdom.

and beyond the reach of its increasingly bellicose neighbors in Thailand. What is unclear is whether this retreat took place with the great pomp and ceremony described by certain chroniclers, or whether the king and his court fled in disarray before the advances of a Thai army. One thing is certain: Angkor was plundered and devastated and, except perhaps for a very short period during the 16th century, was never again to house the capital of Cambodia, which was eventually established at Phnom Penh.

The Thais in Angkor

A late Cambodian chronicle (there are in fact no early ones) gives a polite account of the conqueror's exploits in Angkor, describing the Thai king questioning the "Khmer mandarins" about the origin, history, and purpose of the various monuments he encounters. Having set up a guard to protect the city, "He removed the august statues of the Buddha made of gold, silver, bronze, and precious stones, as well as a number of statues of the August Bull and of other animals." He also invited the monks to follow him and, for good measure, deported to Thailand sixty thousand families from the conquered capital.

By transporting Angkor's statues to his own capital the Thai king was not setting a precedent for Napoleon Bonaparte pillaging Europe to enrich the Louvre: It was not beauty he was removing, but the power of the kings of Angkor as contained in these divine images. A hundred years later the Burmese were shrewd enough to do the same: When they conquered Thailand they sacked Ayuthaya, the

B elow left: Three-headed elephant dating from the 12th or 13th century. Like the other statues now in Mandalay, plundered by the Thais and then by the Burmese, it probably came from Neak Pean, Chou Ta-kuan's "island in the Northern Lake" at Angkor.

R ight: A late-19th-century colored engraving showing how the Bayon might once have looked. Chou Ta-kuan described the temple as a "golden tower flanked by more than twenty stone towers and by several hundred stone chambers," but failed to mention the faces on the towers.

capital, and in their turn removed a number of the Angkor statues. Finally in 1734 these statues arrived in Mandalay, where they have remained ever since.

Around the Middle of the 16th Century the King of Cambodia, Hunting for Elephants in the North of the Country, Discovered a Vast Abandoned City Overgrown by Tropical Forest

The king had the site cleared and installed his court there. News of this event was spread in Europe at the beginning of the 17th century through publications compiled from accounts by Portuguese missionaries. It is clear from even

A bove: The route taken by the Khmer bronzes looted by the Thais in 1431.

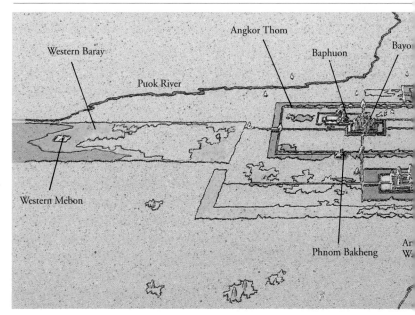

Western Baray

Angkor Thom

Baphuon

Bayo

Puok River

Western Mebon

Phnom Bakheng

An
W

the crudest and most fanciful of these descriptions that the city in the jungle was in fact the "Walled City," "Angkor-the-Great," rediscovered in around 1550 or 1570 and visited by a few missionaries or adventurers. It was not Angkor Wat, where numerous inscriptions testify to the pious activity of a variety of donors at around the same time; the great temple, originally devoted to the worship of Brahma, had by then become the Buddhist sanctuary that it has remained to this day.

Western Interest in Cambodia

In the Age of Discovery Cambodia held little interest for the West. It was not on the trade routes handling gold or spices; it was neither powerful nor rich and had little to offer either merchant or conquistador. Just a few traders, adventurers, and missionaries stopped off there from the middle of the 16th century; at the end of the century their numbers

Accounts by 16th-century European voyagers mention Angkor Thom's navigable canals but not the artificial lakes.

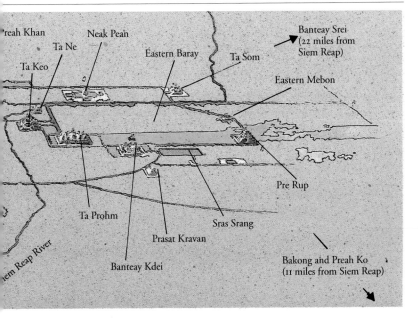

Preah Khan · Ta Ne · Neak Pean · Ta Keo · Eastern Baray · Ta Som · Banteay Srei (22 miles from Siem Reap) · Eastern Mebon · Pre Rup · Ta Prohm · Sras Srang · Prasat Kravan · Banteay Kdei · Bakong and Preah Ko (11 miles from Siem Reap) · Siem Reap River

increased, when the kings of Cambodia appealed for aid from the Portuguese in Malacca and later the Spanish at Manila. Though fruitless, the Spanish expeditions drew attention to Cambodia. Chapters of books and entire volumes were devoted to the country, and Angkor Thom duly figured in these accounts. Soldiers of fortune and traders were not writers, but their stories got around, and missionaries often sent their superiors detailed letters.

Portuguese and Spanish compilers reproduced these accounts, learning through them of the existence of the Walled City, "an exceptional phenomenon which may be regarded as one of the Wonders of the World," as one of them put it. They were torn between admiration and disbelief, another of them admitting that he had balked at describing what seemed like the "fantastic city of Plato's *Atlantis* or of his *Republic*," but that he had been swayed by the irrefutable evidence provided by the men of God. Throughout these early publications, admiration and amazement are equally matched.

The area as it is today, with most of the lakes, or *barays*, and canals (shown in blue or tan) filled in. The site covers some thirty-one miles east–west, but the principal monuments are built along the channeled Siem Reap River. At the north, surrounded by a large square moat, is Angkor Thom, the last of the cities here; to the south is Phnom Bakheng, thought to be the center of the original Angkor (of which only the southwestern section of the moat remains, silted up). Further south still lies the vast temple of Angkor Wat.

The City Rediscovered

The city is described by these writers as a beautiful fortress of immense size, measuring four leagues in circumference. The fortifications, they say, are most extraordinary, the stones (sometimes fancifully said to be of polished marble, though really of rough laterite) being perfectly joined without the use of mortar. The glacis, or slope, on the inner side is accurately noted, but the tops of the walls are given crenellations, a European feature, with merlons in the shape of various animals. The gates are said to be splendid, though no mention is made of the faces surmounting them; and the roadways leading from each of these gates across the moat excite much speculation, their gods and demons—Chou Ta-kuan's "stone generals"—being frequently described as atlantes.

Descriptions of the interior of the city are limited to such observations as "beautiful houses built of stone and laid out in streets in an orderly fashion," "streets paved with marble slabs," and "monuments made of alabaster and jasper." Some writers mention a "former royal palace" or, in the center of the city, "a most extraordinary unfinished temple" or a "great temple with idols"—no doubt the Bayon, although it seems odd that, like Chou

Above: One of the Angkor Thom causeways with its "openwork stone parapets...on which there are stone giants" (Diogo do Couto).

Below: Angkor Wat lion.

Ta-kuan, they fail to mention the faces on the towers. Others refer to the existence in the city of a "temple with five peaks," by which they appear to mean Angkor Wat, the vast temple situated outside the walls.

There were so many marvels to describe within the city that the surrounding area tended to be forgotten. Angkor Wat, though a hive of activity at this date, can be identified with certainty from only two texts, of which one, based by the early 17th-century Portuguese chronicler Diogo do Couto on a description of the 1580s by a Capuchin friar, was not published until much later. As to other monuments in the vicinity, Diogo do Couto only mentions "numerous temples that seem to have been the tombs of the lords of these kingdoms," just as Angkor Wat served as "tomb to the kings who built it."

In endeavoring to describe strange monuments they had never seen, the compilers of books based on travelers' tales were doing something not dissimilar to the 17th-century painter Monsù Desiderio's efforts to visualize hell (above). The texts are uneven, often brief, and vague. Yet some of the details are surprisingly precise, indicating a serious approach on the part of the original observers.

[Khmer inscription text]

So Who Did Build the City?

The account of Diogo do Couto, which provides an explanation of the nature and purpose of the monuments, is the only one to give a relatively straightforward account of the city's history. We are told that the walls carry inscriptions in Indian script indicating that it was built "on the orders of twenty kings," and that "seven hundred years were devoted to the task."

No other writers were able to decipher the inscriptions. Instead they put forward hypotheses drawing on classical and Old Testament history, referring to Alexander the Great, the Romans, Trajan, and, in one case, Chinese Jews. Clearly none of them believed that Angkor could have been built by the Cambodians they saw around them—a prejudice that resurfaced in the 19th century, reinforcing the sense of mystery that had accrued to the place.

Awareness of a Great Heritage

Despite the ignorance attributed to them by outsiders, the Cambodians themselves had no doubt that it was the king's ancestors who had built Angkor Thom and Angkor Wat.

In the 16th century Angkor Wat tended to be called after its royal builder, Suryavarman II (c. AD 1113–50), and it was in his name that the Cambodians completed various bas-reliefs around 1550—a fine example of historical continuity. In the 20th century the completion of these reliefs was at first attributed to Chinese craftsmen—a view proposed by an art historian, based on stylistic considerations, but not unrelated to the notion that post-Angkor Cambodians would have been incapable of such workmanship.

Rubbing of an inscription in the temple of Lolei, made by the Doudart de Lagrée mission in the 1860s. Khmer inscriptions are written in an Indian-based script and are in Sanskrit or a cross between Khmer, Sanskrit, and Pali. It is not clear whether Diogo do Couto knew about the connection with India or whether he was simply relying on inspired guesswork.

Below: The royal barge (1688).

The Heathens' Rome and the Indians' Babel

Cambodian sources say nothing of the "discovery" of the city and its temporary reoccupation by the court. At most the chronicles refer to the installation of King Ang Can in the "province of Angkor Wat," underscoring the fact that the region's center of gravity had shifted away from the Walled City and toward the huge temple situated outside the walls. The inscriptions scarcely mention Angkor Thom, and none of the events they commemorate took place there. It was at Angkor Wat, now "completed" and restored, that statues were installed and offerings were made, and it was to Angkor Wat that pilgrims came from Cambodia, Thailand, and Japan. The city may have ceased to be the capital of the kingdom, but the neighboring temple had become its spiritual heart.

The rare visitors from the West in the 17th and 18th centuries noted the fact. In a 1668 letter a French missionary, one Father Chevreuil, writes that Angkor Wat "is renowned among the Gentiles [heathens] of five or six kingdoms, as Rome is among the Christians." The kings of neighboring countries went on pilgrimages to

Diogo do Couto, author of the 17th century's most accurate description of Angkor. Through an unfortunate set of circumstances his account, which should have appeared in 1614, was not published until 1958.

Angkor even in time of war, and the king of
Thailand sent his emissaries there each
year. Another French missionary, who
visited Angkor around 1783, speaks in
a letter of the "Indians' Babel, a
center of superstition."

The First Plan of Angkor Wat

In 1911 a Japanese professor of civil engineering at
the University of Tokyo, en route to Hanoi, paid a
visit to the Ecole Française d'Extrême-Orient (the
French School in the Far East, an institute for
archaeological research), where he was shown various
documents relating to Angkor. He was intrigued by
the plan of Angkor Wat and in particular by the
large cruciform platform, whose layout, he was told,
"is unique to this monument." He remembered having
seen something similar in Japan in an ancient plan
of an unidentified building, and on his return to
Tokyo he succeeded in locating the document. It
proved indeed to show the great Angkor Wat itself
and turned out to be the oldest plan of an Angkor
monument, drawn in the early 17th century by a
Japanese pilgrim and copied in 1715.

The presence of Japanese merchants in Cambodia and
Thailand at the beginning of the 17th century is well
known and may explain how a pious Japanese Buddhist
could have made his way to Angkor and returned home
with the elements of a plan of the great temple. What is
perhaps more surprising is the confusion that seems to
have arisen between Angkor Wat and the monastery of
Jetavana, one of the holy places associated with the life of
the Buddha in India. In traveling to Angkor our Japanese
pilgrim may in fact have thought he was following in the
footsteps of the Buddha. India was a long way away and
sufficiently unfamiliar to Japanese Buddhists at the
beginning of the 17th century for them to have
mistakenly imagined that Magadha (now Bihar), the
cradle of Buddhism, was situated in what we know as
Thailand and Cambodia. Arriving at "Magadha," our
pilgrim would have headed straight for the marvelous
monastery of which he had heard so much. Spurred on

Model of
Angkor Wat
made for the Colonial
Exposition in
Marseilles (1922).

Opposite: 1715 copy of
a map of Angkor
Wat drawn by a Japanese
pilgrim in c. 1623–36. No
names relating to Angkor
or even to Cambodia
appear in the key to the
map, which situates the
complex in India,
identifying it instead
with the "monastery of
Jetavana." In addition to
the general layout and the
monument's western
orientation—a peculiarity
of Angkor Wat—certain
notes prove the
identification
conclusively. The
reference to "relief
sculptures: four gods
pulling a rope," for
example, is a clear
allusion to the Churning
of the Ocean of Milk
depicted on the wall of
the western gallery (even
if there are in fact more
than four gods).

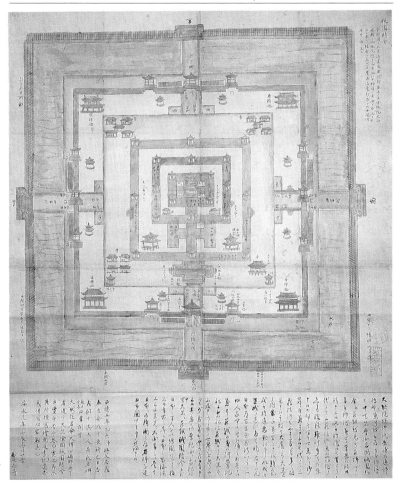

by his faith, he would have had no difficulty recognizing the Jetavana of the old Chinese texts and, though the first Chinese pilgrims spoke of the monastery's decayed condition, he may simply have marveled at finding intact what others had imagined to be ruined.

Thus it is to a combination of geographical ignorance and profound faith that we owe this first illustration of Angkor.

The pilgrim's rough sketch would almost certainly have been tidied up by a professional before being recopied.

"Our readers have been able to form their own opinion of Mouhot's fascinating journals and his extensive portfolio of beautiful drawings. In the three years he spent traveling in Cambodia and the provinces of Siam, Mouhot covered no less than eight hundred leagues. All in all his is one of the most extensive and most informative records Europe possesses on the Indochinese peninsula."

Vivien de Saint-Martin,
Le Tour du Monde, 1863

CHAPTER II
THE "DISCOVERER"

Opposite: Engraving of Angkor Wat from an 1863 copy of a drawing by Henri Mouhot. Below: A portion of his journal.

Angkor as Seen from Bangkok

When in 1819 the Sinologist Abel Rémusat published his translation of Chou Ta-kuan, Europeans knew next to nothing about Cambodia, and still less about Angkor. And yet opportunities existed for gathering information, especially since a number of French missionaries had taken up residence in the province of Battambang, not far from Angkor. They had occasionally visited the city, but their letters—like the one that spoke of the "Indians' Babel"—remained buried in private archives.

In the 1820s Thailand was opening its doors to Europe and there was a thriving Western community in Bangkok. Thailand's annexation of the Cambodian provinces of Battambang and Angkor in 1794 no doubt strengthened relations between the Thai court and the great temple, and one might expect the reports sent from Bangkok regarding Thailand and its possessions to be well documented. This does not appear to have been the case, however, judging by the *Description du Royaume Thai ou Siam* (Description of the Thai Kingdom or Siam) of 1854, which was considered the best Western work on the country. Its author, Monsignor Jean-Baptiste Pallegoix, a scholar and missionary, had spent a great deal of time in the region, but the few lines he devotes to the

"marvelous ruins of Nokorvat" (the Thai name for Angkor Wat) combine a brief reference to the Cambodian legends regarding the origin of the temple with a vague description of monuments "in chiseled marble"—repeating the error made by the early compilers, from whom Pallegoix had no doubt taken his description.

There were others, however, who were more curious. Several members of the British community in Bangkok ventured as far as the city, and one of their number declared that the unraveling of this "marvelous enigma" was a challenge to the scholarly world. Europe at last had a reason for taking an interest in Angkor.

A Missionary at Large

For Father Charles-Emile Bouillevaux (1823–1913) arriving in Cambodia was something of a liberation, since he had spent the previous two years avoiding religious persecution in Cochin China (today in South Vietnam). The warm welcome he received at the hands of an open-minded people and a benevolent king, and the freedom he

"I felt like one of the early apostles cowering in the catacombs in the company of a few faithful followers, with the sword of the persecutors forever hanging over their heads." This is how Bouillevaux described his first contact with the Christian communities of Cochin China. He was nevertheless luckier than his fellow missionary Pierre Borie, beheaded in Tonkin in 1838 (below).

experienced to practice his religion and to move where he chose must have compensated in large measure for the unresponsiveness of the masses to his mission.

It is not clear how much he knew about Angkor before he arrived, but he was evidently not surprised by what he found. Visiting the temples in the vicinity of Battambang and then Angkor itself, he expressed the admiration of a tourist, but not the surprise of an explorer. If he went to Angkor, it is because that is where one must go "to appreciate the splendors of the ancient civilization of Cambodia." In other words, a visit to Angkor was an obligatory part of any missionary's tour of the region.

December 1850: The First Tourist

Bouillevaux published a short account in 1858 of the two days he had spent in Angkor in 1850. Sixteen years later he was to embellish it with details borrowed from his successors—those very authors he accused of taking the credit for discovering Angkor. Traveling upriver from the Great Lake, he passed through the small modern town of Siem Reap, and cut through the jungle to emerge at Angkor Wat's western causeway. Once he had passed the moat and the great entrance pavilion, he was unable to conceal his admiration. Though struck by the strangeness of the place, he found it "imposing, magnificent." He indicated the differences between a Buddhist temple and a Christian church and noted the existence of "other statues of Indian divinities" alongside the statues of the Buddha—

Charles-Emile Bouillevaux (above) felt perfectly at home in Cambodia. For two years he toured the country studying its language and customs as he visited fellow missionaries. Traveling up the Mekong, he spent some time with the mountain dwellers ("Savages"), finding them easier to convert than the Buddhist Khmers of the plain, and, crossing the Great Lake, entered the provinces annexed by Thailand—which he, in common with everyone else, still considered part of Cambodia. A fellow missionary introduced him to Angkor's civilization through monuments near Battambang.

Left: Missionaries in Vietnam, 1852.

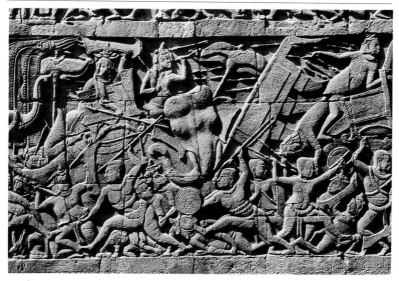

evidence that he was familiar with the technical aspects of religion and, as a good missionary, knew something of heathen gods.

Reaching the walls of Angkor Thom, he stressed the good condition in which he found the southern gate, but it is only in the embellished version of his account that he mentioned the "fifty stone giants": Smothered in vegetation, they had escaped his notice, as they would Henri Mouhot's ten years later.

A similar thing happened regarding his visit to the Bayon. Whereas his first account only mentions the bas-reliefs, in his second version he refers to "immense heads of the Buddha" and an "architectural extravagance ...somewhat reminiscent of the Egyptian style"—a reference to Egypt that is lifted straight out of Henri Mouhot's description of the gates of Angkor Thom.

Bouillevaux concluded with a tourist's nostalgic and weary note (which was in turn borrowed by Mouhot): "There are few things that can stir such melancholy feelings as the sight of places that were once the scene of some glorious or pleasurable event, but which are now deserted."

The reliefs of the Bayon's outer gallery include historic scenes such as this battle between Khmers (bareheaded) and Chams from Vietnam (wearing elaborate headdresses).

"Among the sculptures smothering the walls I saw elephants fighting and men attacking one another with clubs or lances or drawing back their bows and releasing three arrows at once."
Charles-Emile Bouillevaux,
Voyage dans l'Indo-Chine 1848–1856, 1858

The First Images

Armchair travelers around 1860 seeing Angkor through the eyes of Bouillevaux or Chou Ta-kuan were no better off than the early Portuguese and Spanish compilers. They heard repeatedly of marvels and of strange and grandiose sights, but what precisely was this supposed to conjure up in the imagination? The Pyramids, the temples of India, and Chinese pagodas had all been illustrated. Images of Angkor were needed.

It was Henri Mouhot who filled this gap. An enthusiastic explorer and naturalist, Mouhot drew, painted, and even photographed (though unfortunately not in Asia). His journal appeared from 1863 in the review *Le Tour du Monde* and in book form in the Bibliothèque Rose series in 1868. Mouhot's French publishers were quick to exploit the romantic taste for exploration, and what they gave his readers was an emotionally charged account illustrated with a number of remarkable engravings. Most of the meticulous observer's minutely detailed descriptions were consigned to the English edition of his work, published in 1864.

See Angkor and Die

Henri Mouhot was born in 1826 at Montbéliard in eastern France, the son of a treasury employee. At the age of eighteen he was already working as a tutor in a cadet school in Russia, where he traveled extensively before returning home as the Crimean War escalated. He then spent two years exploring Europe with his brother, taking photographs by the daguerreotype method.

In 1856 the two brothers went to England, married the nieces of the Scottish explorer Mungo Park, and settled in Jersey, where Henri devoted himself to his passion for the natural sciences. A recent English work on Thailand gave him the idea of organizing a botanical expedition there. Since he could find no one to subsidize him in France he approached the Royal Geographical Society in London. It entrusted him with a commission but provided no funds, so Mouhot apparently invested the family fortune in the venture and set sail in April 1858. In September

Henri Mouhot drew everything, from peasants in his native France (below) to elephants in Southeast Asia and maps of the areas he explored, but only a handful of his original illustrations are accessible to the public today.

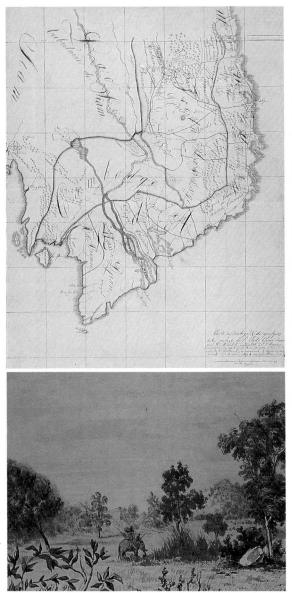

Map showing the land occupied by "Savages" in eastern Cambodia, by Henri Mouhot. The "Savages" Mouhot encountered in Cambodia's eastern mountains were peoples the Cambodians of the plain "still call their elder brothers" and whose characteristics seemed to be "the surviving seeds of an extinct civilization." Mouhot was later struck by seeing their features on Angkor's bas-reliefs and came to the conclusion that these mountain peoples once dominated Indochina. He cited as evidence the tribute regularly paid by the kings of Cambodia and Cochin China to the "fire king" of the Jarai—"this shadow of a king…who seems to have inherited the mantle of the founders of Angkor."

View of the valley of Khao-Koc in Thailand, by Henri Mouhot.

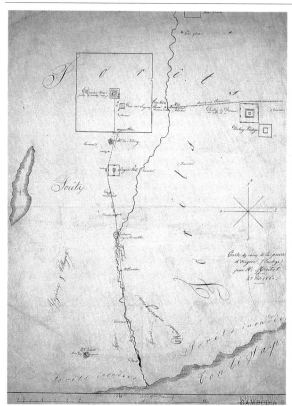

This map of Angkor, which Mouhot (below) drew in 1860—and was not published until 1966—reflects the extent of his investigations. It compares favorably with the more elaborate map drawn a few years later by members of the Doudart de Lagrée expedition and includes most of the principal monuments, some of which, such as Preah Khan and Ta Prohm, are not even mentioned in the French edition of Mouhot's work. The detail here shows Angkor Thom, Angkor Wat (slightly misplaced below it), and to the east Ta Prohm and Banteai Kdei. Errors such as the off-center placing of the Bayon (shown southeast of the royal palace in Angkor Thom) were not to be corrected until the beginning of this century.

he arrived in Bangkok, which was to be the starting point for four separate journeys. The second and longest of these (December 1858–April 1860) took him to Cambodia and to Angkor. The last took him to Laos, where he died of exhaustion on 10 November 1861 somewhere east of Luang-Prabang.

An Unpretentious Naturalist

Although Mouhot was first and foremost a naturalist (a splendid beetle, *Mouhotia gloriosa*, is named after him), he had wide-ranging interests and a passionately inquiring mind. He arrived in Angkor by accident, following the same route as Bouillevaux and guided

by a missionary to whom he said he was enormously indebted. He mentions others who have been there before him and even quotes Bouillevaux himself, making no claim to be breaking new ground with his visit.

By attempting to describe what he "saw and felt" in Angkor, he simply hoped to "contribute to the enrichment of science by extending its field," acknowledging that he knew "nothing" of architecture or archaeology.

Mouhot devoted only a small amount of time to describing and drawing temples, regarding his archaeological essays as "relaxation, a way of resting the body after exerting the mind." This rhinoceros hunt in the Laotian jungle (left) and a scene of monkeys teasing a crocodile in Thailand (below) show how he brought his meticulous animal drawings vividly to life by giving them picturesque settings or incorporating them into a story.

Romanticism and Precision

In the version of his journal that established his reputation in France (as opposed to the book published in England), Mouhot's talent appears to be for drawing and admiring what he saw, rather than for detailed description. However, his lyrical style does not disguise the technical precision of which he was capable. Bouillevaux had dispensed with the "marble" monuments of his predecessors, referring instead to "stone"; Mouhot went further, distinguishing between sandstone and what he called "ferruginous concretions" (laterite).

As a painter he admired the interplay of lines and colors at Angkor Wat—the brilliant blue of the sky, the green of the jungle, the majestic elegance of the architecture. He admired the labor that had gone into the

The causeway and main entrance to Angkor Wat, after a drawing by Henri Mouhot, 1863. Angkor Wat has always been used as a place of worship and never deteriorated into a picturesque ruin buried in the jungle. Mouhot and others after him gave the majestic temple a classical grandeur.

construction of the monuments, speaking of an "Eastern Michelangelo creating his masterpiece," seeking out "obstacles at every turn, for the sheer glory of overcoming them."

Mouhot was already dead when, in 1862, his letters about Cambodia were read to an assembled gathering at the Royal Geographical Society. In them he says a few words about "Angkor's magnificent ruins," promising to provide a full description, and goes into some detail about Cambodia's natural resources—the different kinds of wood grown there, mines, etc. His findings were published in English in 1864 with a foreword by his brother, who referred to the "vast buildings that he discovered in the interior of Siam and Cambodia." Mouhot's French publishers made no reference to a "discovery" in either the serialized version of the journal

Mouhot was buried in the Laotian jungle, where his tomb was drawn by Louis Delaporte (above). The edited version of his journal made appealing reading for anyone eager to hear about exotic places and to learn something of the background of colonial life. For those whom a military or administrative career brought to Cambodia, Mouhot opened up a whole new world: "For us Europeans," said Jean Moura, the second French government representative in Cambodia, "the existence of these imposing ruins in Cambodia came as a complete revelation."

or in the book. The word continued to be bandied around, however, until the idea that Mouhot had "discovered" Angkor simply became an accepted fact.

An End to Private Exploration

Bouillevaux went as a tourist; Mouhot had the support of a scholarly society, but no financial backing; and the handful of British visitors who visited Angkor before them or at roughly the same time did so on their own. After this point Angkor would begin to be explored in a systematic fashion by teams or individuals in the service of official bodies who organized and financed the expeditions, all of them French. There were still one or two private individuals, however, ready to follow in Mouhot's footsteps, including a German geographer and a Scottish photographer.

A Geographer with an Indian Bias

Adolf Bastian was strictly speaking an ethnographer, rather than a geographer. He carried out a thorough exploration of the Angkor region, visiting many monuments and drawing up the first map to show the monuments of Roluos, southeast of Angkor.

Bastian was also one of the first explorers to make a clear distinction between the temple-mountains and the

In February 1866 John Thomson arrived in Angkor accompanied by an employee of the British consulate in Bangkok and met Doudart de Lagrée. He took about thirty photographs of Angkor Wat, including the first panoramic view of its western facade (above). At the Bayon he was fascinated by the face-towers gradually emerging from their shroud of vegetation.

temples "on the flat," which he believed to be palaces. His greatest contribution, however, was to suggest a number of Indian parallels to explain the origin of Khmer architecture and iconography.

The First Photographer

John Thomson (1837–1921) spent ten years photographing the landscapes, monuments, and people of east Asia and was well informed about the places he visited (he had read Chou Ta-kuan, for example). He compares Angkor Wat with temples he had seen in China and especially Indonesia and suggests that the Khmer temple-mountains symbolize the cosmos as described in Indian texts: The central pyramid represents Mount Meru, the axis of the world in Buddhist belief, and the surrounding moat the primordial ocean. Experts were later to take up his ideas and develop them further.

On his return to Europe, Thomson showed his work and a plan he had drawn of Angkor Wat to the British architectural historian James Fergusson, who knew the publications of Mouhot and Doudart de Lagrée, and included an illustrated section on Khmer architecture in his history of world architecture. Khmer buildings, once known only to a handful of enthusiastic amateurs, had at last been brought to the attention of an expert.

> "To the historian of art the wonder is to find temples with such a singular combination of styles in such a locality—Indian temples constructed with pillars almost purely classical in design, and ornamented with bas-reliefs so strangely Egyptian in character."
> James Fergusson,
> *History of Indian and Eastern Architecture*,
> 1876

"From the top of that pagoda I looked down over an immense expanse of fertile countryside." These words were spoken by Vice-Admiral Louis-Adolphe Bonard, governor of Cochin China under French Emperor Napoleon III, and referred to the view that lay before him when he climbed to the fourth level of Angkor Wat in September 1862. But what exactly was he doing there?

CHAPTER III
EXPLORATION

The main entrance to Angkor Wat, in an engraving after Louis Delaporte (opposite), and one of the entrances to the gallery of bas-reliefs, in an engraving after Henri Mouhot.

After the Summer Palace Was Sacked

When Henri Mouhot visited Angkor around 1860, Europe had already begun opening up China to free trade and establishing treaty ports. Indochina, on the country's southern flank, was divided into rival states, many of them weakened by conflict, and offered a means of access to the very heart of the empire. France, which had a military presence in Annam (eastern Indochina) protecting the interests of its missionaries and merchants

The arrival of Vice-Admiral Bonard at the French mission's lodgings in Hue was featured in *L'Illustration* in 1863. *L'Illustration* was one of several periodicals that helped form French public opinion regarding the country's colonization of Indochina. The official organ of the colonial lobby was the *Revue Maritime et Coloniale*.

there, now installed its troops at the mouth of the Mekong in Cochin China. Upriver, the route to China was barred by Cambodia; west of Cambodia was Thailand, where a rival English presence was already established. Cambodia was an obvious French target, and scarcely three months after the conquest of Cochin China the governor of that new French colony was in Angkor.

Bonard's visit to Angkor Wat made one thing quite clear to him: It was no longer possible "to deny that the pitiful Cambodia of today once nurtured and can still nurture a great nation, a nation both artistic and industrious." His conclusion was significant, providing an argument for installing a French military presence in Cambodia. It explains the official interest shown in Angkor from an early date and anticipates the attitude that saw Angkor, and in particular Angkor Wat, as a symbol of colonial rule restoring a nation to its past grandeur.

Vice-Admiral Bonard was the first of the admirals to "reign" over Indochina in the second half of the 19th century. His visit to Angkor was reported in the *Revue Maritime et Coloniale* in 1863, before the appearance of Mouhot's account in *Le Tour du Monde*. Bonard seems only to have visited Angkor Wat, whose "lacework and sculptures" reminded him of Napoleon III's Louvre, just being completed. The transition from one precinct to another suggested to him a progression toward the divine: "It is clear that the worshiper penetrating the temple was intended to have a tangible sense of moving to higher and higher levels of initiation."

A Treaty Was Signed in 1864, Turning Cambodia, and With It Angkor, into a French Protectorate

France officially renounced control of the provinces that had been annexed by Thailand in 1794, but they were not returned to Cambodia until 1907. Even though Angkor was not strictly theirs, the French were in a good position to study and write about it and to use it as a pawn to defend their unpopular colonial policies in Europe.

Relations with Thailand were strained, and the Thai king appears to have been particularly attached to the former Cambodian capital and its temples, and yet, surprisingly, the French move seems to have caused no repercussions there.

France's age-old rivals, the British, were firmly ensconced in neighboring Bangkok, so when the photographer John Thomson arrived in Angkor in the company of a British diplomat the French took an anxious interest in their activities. Their one great fear was that the British might outmaneuver them—not just in Angkor, but, more importantly, in China, their ultimate goal.

Plans Were Made to Explore the Mekong

A project was formulated to investigate whether the river was navigable and whether it offered a viable means of access to China. In 1866 the Mekong Exploration Commission was set up, headed by Ernest Doudart de Lagrée (1823–68), France's representative in Cambodia since 1863. One of the Commission's tasks was to "establish the boundaries of former Cambodia according to tradition and the position of the principal ruins." In order to familiarize the other members of his team with the monuments in question, Doudart de Lagrée arranged for them to make a short detour via Angkor (which he alone had visited) before beginning their journey upriver. He died two years later at Yunnan in southern China. His second in command, Francis Garnier (1839–73), led the last part of the expedition, and in 1873 oversaw publication of the report of their findings.

Doudart de Lagrée (below) had visited Angkor on two occasions before taking charge of the Mekong Exploration Commission in 1866. The first accurate plans of Angkor's temples date from this time and were drawn up with the help of Laederich, a meticulous technician and draftsman. Until recently, in fact, the only published plans of many of Angkor's principal monuments were those done by Laederich for Doudart de Lagrée and later Delaporte.

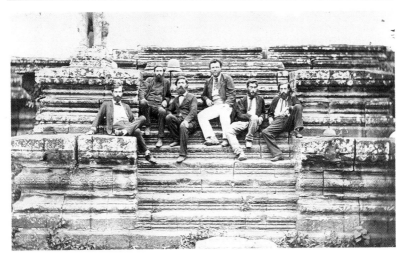

A Team at Work

Doudart de Lagrée had studied at the Ecole Polytechnique and then joined the navy. Arriving in Cambodia in 1863 with a small fleet of ships and a handful of seamen, he faced the task of preparing King Norodom for the terms of the treaty making Cambodia a French protectorate and, once the treaty had been signed, of overseeing its application. Doudart de Lagrée was an energetic and methodical man, and when he was not carrying out negotiations with the king he spent his time learning Cambodian, collecting ancient chronicles, and exploring the length and breadth of the country with his seamen. The purpose of these trips, which included official "excursions" into the provinces annexed by Thailand, was to make the French presence felt in the region and to gather as much information as possible concerning the new territory. During the recent Crimean War he had taken every opportunity to visit landmarks in Asia Minor associated with Homer, and he was similarly eager that the Commission should explore Cambodia's ruins and monuments.

The Commission was made up of six members. A famous photograph shows them at Angkor Wat. The picture was taken by a man named Gsell, a civilian

Above: The members of the Doudart de Lagrée expedition on the steps of the cruciform platform at the end of the causeway at Angkor Wat in 1866. Left to right: Doudart de Lagrée; the diplomat Louis de Carné, nephew of Admiral de La Grandière, governor of Cochin China; the two naval doctors Clovis Thorel (a botanist) and Eugène Joubert (a geologist); Louis Delaporte, a naval officer, like Doudart de Lagrée and de Carné; and finally Francis Garnier. Meeting John Thomson in Angkor gave Doudart de Lagrée the idea of adding a photographer to his team.

photographer, the only person specifically recruited for Angkor, where he photographed the temples. The other members of the commission were young men of multiple talents: Doudart de Lagrée had been told that the Commission would comprise "men of good will" rather than men of learning, who, "true to their noble disposition, would have been dazed and exhausted within a week."

A Scientific Program

In December 1864 a senior official in Saigon had written to Doudart de Lagrée saying: "I hope that you will go to Angkor and that, following your visit, you will send me a splendid account of a picturesque journey full of vivid incidents and illustrated with beautiful, and as yet unpublished, casts and with details of local color, so that we may win the support of artists and persons of inquiring mind in Europe." In fact there could be no doubt about the meticulous scientific nature of the Commission's archaeological program— or indeed of Doudart de Lagrée's personal approach during the three years he had spent exploring Cambodia, spending, as he put it, "entire days looking, counting and measuring."

The Commission Assembled Its Findings in a Work Entitled *Voyage d'Exploration en Indo-Chine*, the First Collective and Multidisciplinary Study Devoted to Ancient Cambodia

Mouhot had already seen most of the monuments Doudart de Lagrée and his team noted in Angkor, but the French reading public was unaware of the extent of Mouhot's investigations and the authors of the *Voyage d'Exploration en Indo-Chine* (Exploratory Voyage in Indochina) appeared to have "discovered" temples that were "forgotten" at the time Mouhot's work was published. Neither Mouhot nor Doudart de Lagrée, however, saw the artificial lakes known as *baray* mentioned by Chou Ta-kuan. On the other hand the *Voyage* does describe the three great temples at Roluos, whose existence had been reported by the German explorer Bastian.

Above: Poster advertising the *Voyage d'Exploration en Indo-Chine*, 1873.

Right: A chromo-lithograph from the *Voyage*, showing Annamese and Cambodians. The *Voyage* is in the grand tradition of the *Description of Egypt* (1809–22) commissioned by Napoleon. Its text in two large volumes comprises an illustrated account of the Commission's journey and a series of appendixes including meteorological observations, a Cambodian glossary, and so on. In addition, there is a magnificent large-format *Atlas* in two parts: A collection of "scientific" documents (route maps, plans and elevations of buildings) and the *Album Pittoresque*, based on watercolors and wash drawings of peoples and places by Louis Delaporte.

Where the team clearly broke new ground was in its investigations outside Angkor. On several occasions during his travels, Doudart de Lagrée had crossed the vast region that lies to the north of the Great Lake, between Angkor and the Mekong. He was thus able to recognize the ancient road that leads out of Angkor to the east, along whose length a number of monuments are situated, notably Beng Mealea and the Great Preah Khan, some sixty miles away (also known as the Preah Khan of Kompong Svay or Preah Khan of Kompong Thom, to distinguish it from the Preah Khan just north of Angkor Thom).

Further east, not far from the Mekong, the temple of Wat Nokor is described in the *Voyage* under the name of Phnom Bachei. Finally, in the course of their journey upriver, the Commission visited the temple of Wat Phu, built on a mountainside in southern Laos. Theirs are the first illustrations we have of it.

Drawing on this impressive body of material,

Louis Delaporte produced the official drawings for the Commission. Despite his preference for picturesque views and imaginative reconstructions, images like the one below, of Angkor Wat's western approaches, are also essentially accurate. Delaporte left nothing out—elephants, vegetation, the sailor-artist at work with an inquisitive villager peering over his shoulder.

Doudart de Lagrée and Garnier summarized their findings in an introduction to the chapters on archaeology in the *Voyage*. It was not until a century later that the first archaeological handbook on Cambodia appeared, but the Commission had already produced a very creditable outline for such a work.

Artists' Impressions

The plans and sections illustrating the text vary in quality. Those of monuments situated outside Angkor were produced in the course of brief visits and were not checked for accuracy. The Angkor illustrations are better: Those of Angkor Wat, for example, include a fine elevation by Laederich, and there is a good cross section of the Bakheng by the same draftsman. Most of Louis Delaporte's "views," on the other hand, are reconstructions with, in some cases, a strong imaginative element. Taken together, however, and including the drawings of decorative details and Gsell's photographs,

Bouillevaux, Mouhot, and many others describe their surprise on emerging from the jungle to see Angkor Wat spread out before them—its causeway in the foreground spanning a wide moat, then the long terrace with its triple entrances, and beyond it a vast open space with, in the distance, the five towers looming over the long gallery of bas-reliefs.

Variations on the Bayon

❝As you stand in this enclosed space you see forty-two towers of varying dimensions rising up on all sides. In the center is a tower which is taller than the rest. Carved on each of the towers are four colossal human faces gazing out toward the four cardinal points. The number of towers and their precise arrangement can be grasped only after several attempts.**❞**
Doudart de Lagrée,
Voyage d'Exploration en Indo-Chine, 1873

Delaporte illustrated Doudart de Lagrée's description of the Bayon with two very different views, both of them printed in the *Voyage*. In the first—seen here—the Bayon, standing on a massive platform and surrounded by a moat (both imaginary), is represented as a fortress bristling with pinnacles so slender that the faces have entirely lost the colossal dimensions described in the text.

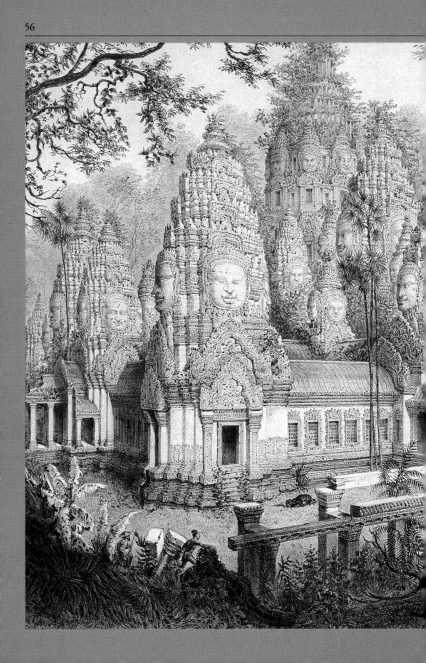

The Bayon with Tiger

Delaporte's second view of the Bayon appeared in the *Album Pittoresque* of the *Voyage*. The jungle is dense and mysterious and Delaporte includes a tiger crossing the temple courtyard. In front lie the ruins of a gallery; behind, the Bayon rears up in all its colossal majesty, still virtually intact (despite the plants that have taken root on its towers). In overall effect this view is closer to the real Bayon than the first, but even here the windowed gallery and the porches at the foot of the towers have been taken from Angkor Wat. (Even stranger things were to happen in the Indochinese Museum displays in Paris.)

the illustrations in the *Voyage* gave readers a reasonably accurate idea of the monuments discussed in the text.

First Attempts at a Chronology

While Delaporte might mix different styles, the authors of the *Voyage* were not unconcerned with the idea of evolution in Khmer art. Like Mouhot, they were interested in how the primitive and the decadent framed a moment of classical perfection, but occasionally their aesthetic reactions were based on historical considerations. Since Chou Ta-kuan did not specifically mention Angkor Wat (he called it the "tomb of Lu Pan"), they concluded that the great temple must have been built after the end of the 13th century. (In fact, it dates from the 12th century.) Conversely, when they investigated the Bayon, which did appear in the Chinese traveler's accounts, they were convinced that it must predate Angkor Wat; but they noted that "nevertheless, to judge by the careful execution manifest in certain details and the tendency to cover the walls with sculpture, we are clearly dealing with a fully mature art."

The Bayon was not placed in its proper position in the history of Cambodian art (between 1177 and 1230) until 1920, but the authors of the *Voyage* did recognize that the Khmers had produced "one of the most original and most powerful styles of architecture." They concluded: "The dual inspiration that links Cambodian art with Greek architecture on the one hand and Gothic architecture on the other, while it cannot set it on a par with either, ought perhaps to rank its productions immediately behind the greatest masterpieces of the West." Europe could breathe a sigh of relief. The artistic hierarchy was intact: The new territories might encompass great marvels, but none could rival its own.

Martyrs, Colonial Feelings, and Scientific Interest

The expedition was a failure in economic terms. France had hoped to flood the Chinese market with French

Francis Garnier (left) was an energetic and courageous man (though not popular with Doudart de Lagrée) who had planned a journey up the Mekong with a dentist friend in 1863 and on his own explored the area north of Angkor. He also wrote an essay on the history of Cambodia and translated the royal chronicles assembled by Doudart de Lagrée. He met his end in Tonkin in 1873 (below).

imports via the Mekong River, but the project proved unrealizable, as the river was barely navigable. The expedition also had its martyrs: Doudart de Lagrée for one, but also Louis de Carné, who died in 1871, and Francis Garnier, killed in Tonkin in 1873 by Chinese-backed "Black Flag" pirates. France was weakened by the Franco-Prussian War and now regarded the Indochinese venture with some uncertainty. Appearing when it did, in 1873, the *Voyage* was able to show that there were other gains to be made in Indochina beyond the military and the commercial.

Doudart de Lagrée's tomb at Tong-Chuen in the Chinese province of Yunnan, erected by Garnier.

Scholars, the very men who had been excluded from the expedition, were stirred into action. In a report to the minister for the navy, the Académie des Inscriptions et Belles-Lettres demanded that serious measures be taken to preserve monuments situated in a territory henceforth protected by France. With the appearance of the

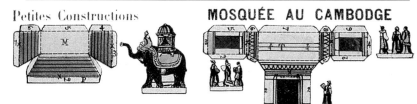

Petites Constructions
MOSQUÉE AU CAMBODGE

Voyage and the examination of documents brought back by the Commission, it became clear that Mouhot's wish had been met and that a new area of interest had opened up to European science. In 1865 the scholarly *Revue Archéologique* had published an account simply lifted from a Saigon newspaper. That was no longer enough.

Garnier and de Carné had already described their first impressions in other more widely read journals. The conclusion of both was that the West had barely begun to unravel the mystery of Angkor. "Who, in short, are the real creators of Angkor-the-Great and to what race do they belong?" asked Garnier, while de Carné noted: "These tombs seem too beautiful for the race that lies buried in them."

Three-Dimensional Reconstructions

The first casts of details from Angkor were made by Doudart de Lagrée. The other members of the Commission then went on to make a great many more, and their collective works were shown at the Universal Exhibition in Paris in 1867 and later transferred to the permanent colonial exposition. The public could now literally see and touch the mysterious ruins it had previously only known through Mouhot's drawings.

The displays proved a great attraction, a fact not lost on the organizers, and with each subsequent exhibition new examples were added to the existing collection. At first they were simply sculptural details, but individual pieces were soon assembled to reproduce entire structures. Delaporte's reconstructions at the Indochinese Museum in Paris confirmed the success of the technique, which achieved its high point with the gigantic models of Angkor Wat shown at the colonial expositions in the 20th century.

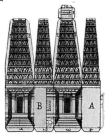

Above: Cut-out paper model of a "Cambodian mosque," early 20th century.

Cambodia comes to France. Opposite: A hybrid temple in the former Indochinese Museum in Paris. In 1866 Doudart de Lagrée had used plaster casts to supplement fragments of sculpture brought back from his early explorations and held a successful display at Saigon. Ten years later Delaporte had the brilliant idea of making schematic models that incorporated genuine casts. The result was a mixture of heterogeneous elements true to the spirit of Khmer architecture that did not represent an actual building.

At the Universal Exposition of 1867 in Paris, vast crowds jostled among stone giants and monsters. A colossus with five heads and ten arms clutched a dragon with nine heads, while a rearing lion stretched out its claws, ready to pounce. All around the casts there were plans and especially drawings, which showed rafts laden with stone figures careening down torrential rivers overhung with vines.

CHAPTER IV
THE LAST OF THE EXPLORERS

As the Khmers had used water to transport stone, so Louis Delaporte used it to remove sculptures (opposite). Right: Members of the Delaporte expedition, 1874.

A New Lord Elgin En Route to Tonkin

During his time in Cambodia as a member of the Mekong Exploration Commission, Louis Delaporte (1842–1925) became a great admirer of Doudart de Lagrée, whose memory he staunchly defended, and Khmer art, to which he was to devote the rest of his life. When he was put in charge of an exploratory mission to Tonkin, Delaporte obtained authorization to begin the expedition in Cambodia— and in fact he never left. The specific objective of the mission was something new: to visit monuments with a view to bringing statues and other sculptures back to France, thereby assembling the first official collection of Khmer art. Delaporte went further than that, continuing Doudart de Lagrée's initiatives and visiting sites his predecessor had described or mentioned in passing. Delaporte had a large team at his disposal and they collected statues, drew up plans (Laederich had joined this expedition too), copied lintels, and prepared reconstructions. At the Great Preah Khan he found abundant

Above: A member of the Delaporte mission. Louis Delaporte, the mainspring of the Universal Exposition in Paris, had traveled to Mexico and Iceland before being selected for the Doudart de Lagrée expedition for his cartographic and drawing skills. Director of the Indochinese Museum until his death in 1925, he was passionate about Khmer art, but also conscious of his limitations, saying to George Coedès in 1909: "I am only half a curator. I have only focused on art. Others will do the rest!"

Left: Sculptures from the Preah Khan at Angkor at the Universal Exposition in Paris, 1878. Here the general public had its first real exposure to Khmer art.

Reconstruction of the Preah Ko, from Louis Delaporte's *Voyage au Cambodge*, 1880. This temple is part of the Great Preah Khan complex, situated about sixty miles east of Angkor and dating for the most part from the 12th and 13th centuries, like Angkor Wat and the Bayon. Like Neak Pean, it is built in the center of a *baray*. The animals and human figures piled up at the corners symbolize the different levels of the universe, from the underworld of the *nagas*, or serpents, trampled by elephants, to the celestial world represented by the wild geese with wings spread wide. Delaporte was the first to draw attention to this remarkable monument. Though clumsy, his view captures the building's principal features, despite its ruinous condition.

material and, awestruck, drew the Preah Ko, a building like an enormous sculpture, with a central tower covered with reliefs and flanked at the corners by elaborate groups of elephants and fantastic birds.

At Angkor Delaporte had a huge number of casts made and continued to explore the region, in particular the area north of the city. From the Preah Khan near Angkor Thom he brought back the "giant with five heads and ten arms," and he drew a splendid elevation of Neak Pean, the island temple in Chou Ta-kuan's "Northern Lake."

Angkor in the Museums

Delaporte returned to France with "some seventy pieces of sculpture and architecture" that he claimed to have bought, or rather, traded for. He had gone out to Cambodia with a collection of goods including "a

Overleaf: Statue being transported across the Great Preah Khan swampland—almost certainly the "giant leaning on a club" removed from Preah Ko (left). Clearing the temple of Preah Stung in the Great Preah Khan area (right). The face-tower, resembling those of the Bayon, is a rarity outside Angkor. From Delaporte's *Voyage*, 1880.

number of statues, paintings, and engravings to present to the king and to the mandarins." He made a point of offering some of these goods to King Norodom, explaining with great diplomacy that "our government requested his permission to remove from his States certain artistic treasures to which we attach value and sent him in exchange a number of objects of artistic value from France."

Delaporte's sculptures did not go to the Louvre in Paris, as he had hoped, but were exiled to the château of Compiègne, a former imperial residence for which the Republic had no real use. A few items were transferred to the Trocadéro in Paris for the Universal Exposition of 1878, and there two years later Khmer art acquired a home in the new Indochinese Museum.

Souvenirs from Cambodia

Cambodia's visitors were not all official: The ancient sites also attracted administrators taking a holiday, sailors on leave, and even the more enlightened type of tourist. Angkor and the Great Preah Khan were not obvious choices, since one was in Thailand and the other was relatively inaccessible, and the majority of tourists tended to visit southern Cambodia and Cochin China instead. These visits produced a rich crop of souvenirs: sometimes entire statues, more often heads or small bronzes that were easier to transport. Back in France some of these items ended up in the large museums—the

Trocadéro or the Guimet—or in lesser-known ones like that at Rochefort. A number remained, however, in private homes. While hidden from the view of the general public, they heralded a time when Khmer art would come into its own, offering a passionate focus of interest to collectors and antiquarians.

Angkor at the Salon

Delaporte's drawings opened up a whole new world to

Delaporte was anxious to build up the collections of the Indochinese Museum (now all in the Guimet Museum in Paris). This sandstone statue of Brahma (opposite below), found a few miles from the temple of Wat Baset in the Battambang region, where Bouillevaux and Mouhot first encountered Khmer art, was presented to the Indochinese Museum in 1888. Delaporte himself brought back the heads of Shiva (above) and Brahma (left) from a temple situated on the Phnom Bok northeast of Angkor. The frieze of dancers (opposite above) is from Angkor Wat. When the Cambodian royal dancers visited France in 1906 the public could see just how little Cambodia's artistic traditions had changed.

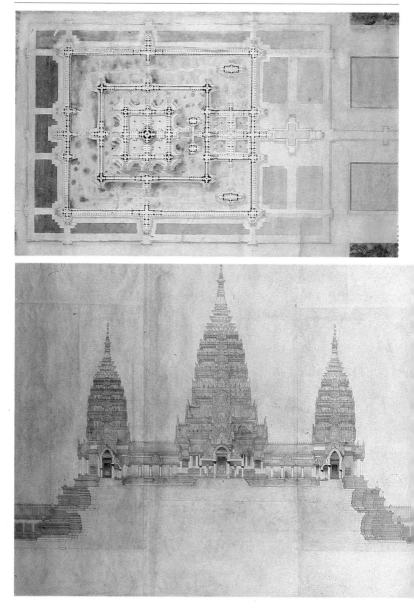

architects back home. Khmer buildings combined what seemed to them to be totally opposing ideas: classical rigor in the overall composition, decorative extravagance, and a complete dichotomy between external forms and internal design. At the time such heterodoxy may have surprised and even shocked some people in Europe, but the general response was one of admiration mixed with astonishment. A few architects, including Lucien Fournereau, made the journey to Angkor to see the monuments for themselves and came home with material for books and articles that explained the basic principles of Khmer architecture, helped familiarize the West with an art foreign to its taste and understanding, and contributed to a richer appreciation of Angkor's architectural achievements.

Encouraged by Delaporte, architect Lucien Fournereau went to Angkor in 1887–8, returning with casts, sculptures, vases, photographs, and—above all —plans, cross sections, and elevations, which he showed at the Salon. As technical achievements his drawings had few rivals before the great campaign of the 1960s. Opposite and below: Plan (with north at the bottom) and restored elevation of Angkor Wat.

Numbering the Monuments

While Delaporte was fighting to bring Khmer art to
public attention, Indologists in Paris continued to study
rubbings sent from Cambodia in an attempt to decipher
the ancient inscriptions.

In Cambodia, meanwhile, lists were being drawn up.
In an effort to reconstruct a complete picture of the
former empire every remaining trace of it was recorded.
It was another naval man, the epigrapher Etienne
Aymonier (1844–1929), who began the job of
inventorying Cambodia's monuments, traveling great
distances to achieve his objectives.

Remains of the bygone empire were still very much a
part of local people's lives, landmarks familiar to villagers
and forest dwellers, who had their own names and
legends. An ancient temple built beside a beautiful
mango tree must naturally be the Prasat Svay, the "Temple of the Mango." A temple standing in the forest near
a village was the Prasat Prei, the "Temple of the Forest,"
or, if it had a wall around it, the Banteay Prei, "Citadel
of the Forest." If its walls were decorated with images
of beautiful young women, it was the Banteay Srei, the
"Citadel of Women." If it housed a fine stone lion, then
it was the Prasat Sing, the "Temple of the Lion."

Unfortunately for archaeologists, however, Cambodia
had its fair share of mango trees, forests, beautiful female
divinities, and stone lions. It was a French military man,
Etienne-Edmond Lunet de Lajonquière, who found a
practical solution to this problem. Sent out to Cambodia
by the new Ecole Française d'Extrême-Orient to continue Aymonier's work, Lajonquière decided to number
every monument, large or small, that he came across. He
listed 910 in total. Angkor Wat continued to be known
as Angkor Wat rather than temple no. 497; but it was
clearly useful to be able to distinguish the Temple of the
Lion no. 365 from the Temple of the Lion no. 410. There
was even a small Angkor Thom temple which, for want
of a better name, came to be known as "Monument 486."

The Assault on the Bayon

The Ecole Française d'Extrême-Orient took a
particular interest in Angkor, commissioning an

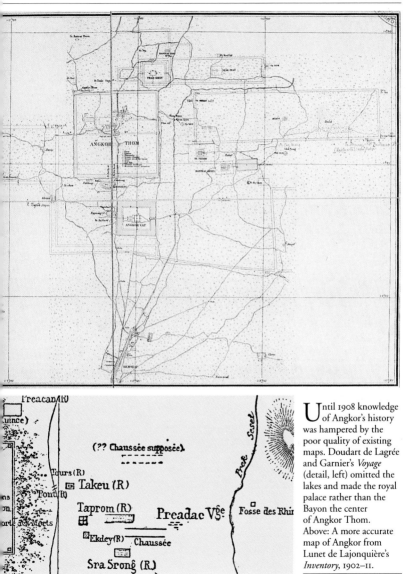

(?? Chaussée supposée).

Tours (R)

Takeu (R)

Pont (R)

Taprom (R)   Preadac Vᵍᵉ   Fosse des Rhin

Ekdey (R)   Chaussée

Sra Srong (R)

Preacan (R)

Prei Secret

Until 1908 knowledge of Angkor's history was hampered by the poor quality of existing maps. Doudart de Lagrée and Garnier's *Voyage* (detail, left) omitted the lakes and made the royal palace rather than the Bayon the center of Angkor Thom. Above: A more accurate map of Angkor from Lunet de Lajonquière's *Inventory*, 1902–11.

Private Memories

The photographs on these and the following pages form part of a large collection taken by a tourist in c. 1890. His friends—and perhaps he himself—are recorded on the Elephant Terrace at Angkor Thom (opposite above), at the ruined entrance of one of the Bayon's galleries, and (with a Cambodian) at a small temple.

Overleaf: The photographer followed the standard route, and many of the pictures he took are classic views like those of a head at the Bayon (above left), and the main entrance to Angkor Wat (right). Others were more unusual, such as a detail of Angkor Thom's southern gate (below left). The heads of the three elephants of Indra, with their long postlike trunks, were collapsing under the pressure of the roots.

architect, Henri Dufour, and a photographer, Charles Carpeaux (son of the sculptor of the famous group depicting *Dance* on the Paris Opera House), to prepare a monograph on one of its most important temples, the Bayon. Carpeaux, who knew the Trocadéro collections well, visited Angkor on two separate occasions and was to die in Saigon in 1904 on his return from his second visit.

Before they could draw up a plan or take casts and photograph the bas-reliefs of the temple's two galleries, an attempt at clearing the site had to be made. Teams of workmen set about removing the rubble using levers and ropes, but the vegetation proved more of a problem. Here and elsewhere banyans and other large trees clung to the ruins; even more pervasive were bushes and scrub. After three years of work, the vegetation was as dense as ever. The task of clearing, deciphering, and understanding begun by Carpeaux was to keep workers busy for years to come.

An Angkor Pilgrim

Carpeaux received a wide circle of friends in Angkor, including an admiral, a famous writer, a less-famous sculptor, a bishop, a doctor and his wife, a number of sailors and soldiers, and even an American globetrotter with a passion for port.

Charles Carpeaux, photographed at one of the Bayon's windows. His vivid notebooks, letters, and photographs provide the best introduction there is to Angkor village life at the beginning of the 20th century. What interested him was everyday events: A festival at Angkor Wat, a family taking a siesta, the writer Pierre Loti doing the same "on a wretched mat," or monks visiting the Angkor mission (left).

On 5 December 1901, he notes, "the bonzes' pope comes to see us accompanied by his vicars. They bring us coconuts."

"18 December 1901. Worked at the Baion [*sic*]. Good day for the School. Cleared part of the N. facade. Found four gray snakes…. Tried to wash the bas-reliefs. They are covered with ancient lichen, which is very stubborn! I shall have to do this work myself using my own chisels. Too delicate for the coolies. Developed three photographs of the towers."

Charles Carpeaux
Les Ruines d'Angkor
1908

When Carpeaux and Dufour arrived, the Bayon's galleries were blocked with fallen masonry, while the bas-reliefs were choked by rubble and vegetation. Carpeaux and Dufour's photographs, which appeared in 1910–4, remain to this day the only accessible record of these reliefs, since Luc Ionesco's photographic survey made in the 1960s has never been published. Seen here are workers moving a large stone (above) and clearing the outer gallery (center), as well as part of the inner precinct (below).

The writer was Pierre Loti (1850–1923), whose account *Un Pèlerin d'Angkor* (An Angkor Pilgrim) of 1912 marked the site's first appearance in a work of literature. Loti met Carpeaux only briefly and had his own personal reasons for visiting Angkor, which had exercised a powerful influence on his imagination since early childhood. He describes how an illustration in a colonial journal had shown him "in the depths of the jungles of Siam…the evening star rising over the ruins of mysterious Angkor." His pilgrimage—three days in November 1901—took him to Angkor Wat and to the Bayon, "one of the most stupendous temples in the world." He was enchanted by the forest that "shrouds the city" and by the shifting effects of light on stone at different times of day and in different weather.

Loti dedicated *Un Pèlerin d'Angkor* to Paul Doumer, governor-general of Indochina, but fundamentally he disapproved of the French occupation of the territory: "This episode will lack grandeur and will above all be short-lived," he said; "soon we will scarcely see any white men wandering about in this region… so idiotically desperate to rule over Asia, which has existed since time immemorial, and to disrupt the course of things there."

The risk that Loti envisaged was that Western interference would disrupt the remarkable continuity that existed between former Cambodia and the Cambodia of King Norodom, a continuity that he perceived all around him—in the piety emanating from Angkor Thom's scattered images or the sculptural groups at Angkor Wat, in the architecture of the current dynasty's royal tombs, where Angkor's art lived on, "though its colossal proportions are reduced," and even more obviously perhaps in the graceful performances of the royal dancers. "We are right in the midst of the Ramayana," Loti wrote, "and Angkor Thom would certainly have witnessed the same entertainments…. Times we thought were forever past are revived before our eyes; nothing has changed here, either in the spirit of the people or in the heart of their palaces."

In 1906 King Sisowat (1906–27), Norodom's successor, visited France accompanied by the royal dancers. Auguste Rodin sketched the king (above) and made a series of drawings of the dancers (opposite) for which he had to pursue them from Paris to Marseilles. "Every human type and every race has its beauty," he wrote in *L'Art* (1924). "It is simply a matter of discovering it. I absolutely loved drawing the little Cambodian dancers who came to Paris with their king. The delicate movements of their slender limbs were strangely, wonderfully seductive."

In 1907 Angkor was returned to Cambodia along with all the provinces annexed by Thailand more than a century earlier. It could never again be the capital of the kingdom, but it was the center of attention. The Cambodians themselves had not forgotten it, but now they got to know it better. Legions of workmen, illustrators, and photographers were freeing it from the jungle, restoring it, and protecting it.

CHAPTER V
ANGKOR REINSTATED

Opposite: King Sisowat at Angkor, with the representative of the French government, c. 1907. Right: A souvenir handkerchief showing the model of Angkor Wat at the Colonial Exposition in Marseilles, 1922.

Now that it was officially back in Cambodia, Angkor automatically came under the control of the Ecole Française d'Extrême-Orient, at that time effectively the scientific arm of French colonial rule. With this change of affairs came "new duties," as the School's director put it. The archaeologists and epigraphists (scientists who study ancient inscriptions) connected with the School found themselves confronted with extra-ordinary, in a sense limitless, possibilities for exercising their skills. At one time missions came and went, but now there was a team permanently at work. This virtual monopoly may have been a source of irritation, but for more than sixty years, as methods changed, it insured a remarkable continuity in the scientific and technical efforts to restore Angkor to its former glory.

Starting in 1912 tour operators offered two-day all-inclusive visits to Angkor. A price list for such a visit is above.

The Arrival of the Tourists

Angkor did not attract only archaeologists. The autumn of 1907 saw an influx of more than two hundred tourists in barely three months, most of them probably colonials from Phnom Penh or Saigon.

A visit to Angkor was not a simple day trip, however. It involved crossing the Great Lake by steam launch to the foot of Phnom Krom, taking a sampan upriver to the small town of Siem Reap, and there exchanging the sampan for a buffalo-drawn cart, a contraption that was light and graceful but not built for comfort, particularly on the poor road leading to Angkor Wat. Often the buffaloes refused to budge and the wheels got stuck in the sand, and a journey that could be done in an hour and a half might take six.

Within the temple enclosure a straw hut on piles served as a hotel, though guests had to bring their own bed linen, cooking equipment, and food. Time was short, since the steamer left for the return journey barely two and a half days after dropping people off and did not return for a whole week. Visiting Angkor Wat itself presented no difficulties. Even though the terraces were

In 1908 the Duc de Montpensier drove from Saigon to Angkor Wat, a feat he crowned by maneuvering his car up the monument's steps. Opposite: Ascending the steps (above); the car on the Angkor Wat causeway (center); the duke's book (1910, below). In 1926 parking restrictions and a speed limit of about eighteen miles (thirty kilometers) per hour were introduced throughout the Angkor site.

overgrown, the galleries were easily accessible and the stairways intact.

Angkor Thom was another matter. The jungle here was more dense and the road inferior, twisting around enormous buttress-like tree roots. The Bayon, with its giant faces looming down from the towers, was a vast crumbling mass of stone festooned with vegetation, and viewing the bas-reliefs frequently involved acrobatics. The area at the base of the Elephant Terrace was often a swamp —Delaporte's reconstruction shows a procession approaching the temple in a dugout canoe!—

DUC DE MONTPENSIER

La Ville au Bois dormant
de Saigon à Angkor en Automobile

LIBRAIRIE PLON

and access to the famous Leper King could be equally awkward. Wherever one went the picture was the same, and not all the new tourists felt capable of following Mouhot's valiant example. The beauty of the monuments called for something better: Mystery should not have to go hand in hand with discomfort.

The Ecole Française d'Extrême-Orient Proposed to "Improve Access and Accommodation for Visitors" and "Insure Conservation and Upkeep of the Buildings"

Improving the means of access to Angkor generally and building a proper road between Phnom Krom and Angkor Wat were the job of the public works department, not archaeologists. Similarly, it was up to the local authorities to install a bungalow for visitors in

1784. Ex-Cambodge – ANGKOR-THOM
Les Tours à quatre visages

the vicinity of Angkor Wat—not in Angkor Wat itself, since if tourism was not to pose a further threat to the temples it had to be properly channeled. The plan was simple: Angkor Wat was to be designated a protected area (the term "Angkor park" was already in use) and an agent from the School's archaeological service was to act as curator.

Men of Multiple Talents

Successive curators at Angkor were all professional men, though none until the last was an archaeologist by training. The first, Jean Commaille (1868–1916), was a

Postcards were produced for tourists. The one on the left features the Bayon towers.

Opposite above: A card issued to visitors by the Ecole Française d'Extrême-Orient, 1933. The school is a research rather than teaching institution. Founded in 1898 as the Archaeological Mission in Indochina, based in Saigon, and later Hanoi, it was controlled by the French colonial government until after World War II. It was then jointly administered for a few years by the three states of former Indochina and France. Since 1954 its headquarters have been in Paris.

Angkor Wat.
Mar. 99

painter who went to Indochina with the French Foreign Legion. He was in Angkor painting in 1898, and was then employed by the public works department in a variety of jobs before becoming curator in 1908. His pioneering work and his life-style—home was a straw hut beside the Angkor Wat causeway—evidently suited him. Not so his wife. Apparently unable to live without her piano, she packed her bags and left. Commaille was murdered in 1916 on the road to Angkor Wat.

Most of Commaille's successors were architects, and all had been working in Indochina for several years before being recruited for the job. Three of them left their particular mark in the period leading up to the Second World War: Henri Marchal, Georges Trouvé, and Maurice Glaize.

Ecole Française d'Extrême-Orient
Conservation d'Angkor

Below: Watercolor of Angkor Wat by Jean Commaille, 1899.

The curator had sole responsibility for managing the Angkor site, which was no small task. His duties included administration, clearing and excavating the area, restoration work, exploration, research, and making drawings, as well as deterring looters and vandals, curbing encroachment, welcoming honored guests, and showing colleagues around and helping them to test their theories. He also wrote guides, articles, and books, as well as regular reports, and, most important of all, an excavation journal, in which he often noted incidents that had very little to do with archaeology.

Occasional Visitors

Every once in a while, the curator's solitary life at Siem Reap was interrupted. When the visitor was the School's director and when that director was an epigraphist, like Louis Finot or, in particular, George Coedès, then it was more than a simple inspection.

Jean Commaille (left) published a guidebook to Angkor in 1912. The work itself is well informed, but the "sketch plan of the Angkor complex" (opposite) drawn to illustrate it, is somewhat selective, showing only a handful of monuments in a whimsically undulating landscape. Angkor Thom is correctly represented, however, and the monuments left out are described in the accompanying text.

Below: A watercolor of the outer gallery of Angkor Wat by Jean Commaille, 1899.

Angkor in Its True Colors

Léon Busy's autochromes on these and the following pages, dating from the 1920s, gave the European public its first accurate glimpse of Angkor's colors. Left: The Towers of the Rope Dancers (Prasat Suor Prat) at the eastern end of the royal square in Angkor Thom.

The statue of the Leper King at Angkor Thom (below) is without doubt the most famous of all Khmer statues. Rather than a king, however, it probably represents Yama, god of the dead.

The Heart of the Temple

For pilgrims in the 17th century, as for those in the 20th, the heart of Angkor Wat was not the tower crowning the pyramid but the gallery of a Thousand Buddhas (opposite), part of the cruciform galleries on the building's second floor where worshipers assembled a vast collection of statues of varying provenance.

Left: Arriving at the Bayon's fourth level the visitor emerges up in the sky, with giant faces on all sides.

George Coedès (1886–1969) devoted his entire life to deciphering Cambodia's inscriptions, and for him a visit to Angkor was a way of bringing the texts to life. It was also an opportunity for him to start his own excavations in the hope of shedding light on the texts and to transmit to the curator—impose upon him, if necessary—the findings of other people not actually living on the spot; at times such research might seem rather futile.

Until the beginning of the 1930s the director of the School's archaeological service, the curator's immediate superior, was the architect Henri Parmentier. Parmentier paid frequent visits to Angkor, supervising the curator's activities, sometimes acting as his deputy, savagely annotating the excavation journal, and carrying out his own excavations and research. Above all he tramped the length and breadth of Cambodia revising Lajonquière's inventory, a task he continued even after retiring. More than thirty years later the inhabitants of remote villages in the northwest still remembered the austere director and his small team of helpers going around measuring, drawing, and lifting stones to look underneath.

Victor Goloubew in 1937 (above). Left: Henri Parmentier in 1925.

Victor Goloubew (1878–1945), one of the School's archaeologists, was a different type of person altogether. A wealthy aristocrat from St. Petersburg, before losing all his money in the revolution in 1917, he had moved in Parisian high society and he knew the sculptor Auguste Rodin personally. As well as having a taste for fashionable life, Goloubew was a highly cultured man who had traveled widely and was passionately curious about the world in general. In 1936 he took Charlie Chaplin and Paulette Goddard on a tour of Angkor's temples. While flying over the Angkor site several years earlier, he had discovered the remains of Yashodharapura, the earliest city at that location. It was built by Yashovarman at the end of the 9th century around the "Central Mountain," Phnom Bakheng. Goloubew's friends nicknamed the city Goloupura.

An Artist at Phnom Penh

While official conservation efforts continued in Angkor, George Groslier, a French painter living in Phnom Penh, was engaged in his own private campaign to reinstate Cambodian art. Like Rodin before him, Groslier was enchanted by the graceful dancers of the king's troupe, whose counterparts he found sculpted on Angkor's walls. If the dancers had not changed, what of the sculptural tradition that depicted them? Polite society in Phnom Penh might regard Cambodia as "lost forever" and its people as "degenerate," but

Goloubew was a friend of Auguste Rodin, who sculpted a bust of his wife. Rodin and Goloubew together wrote a book about Indian sculpture. Goloubew learned aerial photography during World War I and took it up again in 1930 to hunt for the site of the earliest city at Angkor.

Below: The first crane used at Angkor, photographed in 1909 by Jean Commaille.

Groslier and others like him knew better.

While glorifying past splendors, Groslier maintained, the Western world was allowing the traditions of an everyday art to die out, an art which displayed "a remarkably fixed and enduring aesthetic whose continuity can be demonstrated nine times out of ten by reference to bas-reliefs and monuments dating back to the earliest times." Groslier won his case, and under his aegis a new institution, the School of Cambodian Arts, came into being. Here teams of craftsmen were painstakingly taught Angkor's decorative techniques so that they could work in the ancient traditions.

Groslier's justification for taking such measures on behalf of the Khmer craft industry was that tourists needed to be able to buy souvenirs that were neither stolen sculptures nor mass-produced rubbish.

From Jungle to Park

Jean Commaille cleared Angkor Wat before beginning in a small way on Angkor Thom. He opened up the great avenues leading to the five gates, cleared the Bayon's courtyards of rubble—stacking the blocks of stone in huge piles, where his successors would search for missing fragments from the bas-reliefs—and cut down the trees in the square framed by the Royal Terraces.

It was a slow job, one that was never finished: The

George Groslier (above) built the School of Cambodian Arts and the Albert Sarrault Museum (left) at Phnom Penh. Combining the graceful forms of Buddhist monasteries with the delicate decoration of the local temples, they provided a sympathetic setting for statues and fragments of ornament assembled from all over the country. The new museum, seen here in 1935, was the key work and served as a model for many other projects. Groslier died at Phnom Penh in 1945, following an interrogation by the Kampetai. In front of him in the photograph is his son Bernard-Philippe, future curator of Angkor.

"The banyan that springs from the temple of Neak Pean after checking its upward surge with tentacles that thrust through the stone mass surmounting the four lakes, whose muddy water they drink, is the mark of the divinity which reigns in this place. This divinity is responsible for the miracle."

Elie Faure
Mon Périple
(My Wanderings)
1932

Both the tree and the tower in this 1925 photograph were destroyed by a hurricane in 1935. Although a loss in picturesque terms, the incident enabled Maurice Glaize to reconstruct the temple, described by its 12th-century builder as "a lofty island drawing its charm from the lakes [which surround it], cleansing the mud from those sinners who come into contact with it, serving as a boat to cross the ocean of existences" (Preah Khan stele).

In a poster advertising guided tours (left), visitors were offered the contrasting delights of Angkor Wat's classical grandeur and the mysterious faces buried in the jungle at Angkor Thom. Below: A tourist at the giant seated Buddha of Tep Pranam, Angkor Thom.

EXCURSION AUX RUINES
D'ANGKOR

Les départs de Saigon ont lieu une fois par semaine sur les vapeurs de la Compagnie des Messageries Fluviales:

Saigon, depart Jeudi soir.

Phnom-Penh: Arrivée : Samedi matin.
Départ : Dimanche matin.

Angkor: Arrivée : Lundi matin.
Départ : Mercredi.

Retour à Saigon, Vendredi matin.

Départures from Saigon are weekly, by steamers of the Messageries Fluviales Company :

Leave Saigon, Thursday evening

Phnom-penh: Arriv. Saturday morning
Leave Sunday

Angkor: Arriv. Monday morning
Leave Wednesday.

Return Saigon Friday morning

Il est préférable de visiter les célèbres RUINES D'ANGKOR pendant la saison des hautes eaux, du 15 Juillet au 1 février. La durée du voyage, à partir de Saigon est de 10 jours, aller et retour, y compris deux journées de séjour à ANGKOR.

It is preferable to visit the celebrated RUINS of ANGKOR during the water season, from July 15th to of February.
The voyage from Saigon takes there and back, including a stay at ANGKOR.

Les voyageurs descendent à PHNOMPENH, (Grand Hôtel) pendant la journée d'arrêt du vapeur, tous les renseignements désirables et au besoin le personnel et le matériel nécessaires pour un séjour prolongé dans la région des ruines. Les vapeurs des Messageries Fluviales font escale à l'entrée de la rivière de Siemreap. Les voyageurs à destination d'Angkor, sont transbordés sur des sampans et conduits en deux ou trois heures, à travers la forêt inondée, à la petite ville de Siemreap qui se trouve à 30 minutes d'Angkor; à Siemreap on prend une voiture jusqu'à Angkor.

Une salle en maçonnerie (Maison des passagers) contenant 10 chambres meublées de 16 lits et renfermant des annexes a été construite à l'entrée du Grand temple d'Angkor Vat.

L'excursion complète de Saigon à Angkor, séjour compris, revient environ à 100 fr. (250 fr.) par tête.

NOTA. — De Saigon on peut aussi se rendre à Tourane (Grottes de marbre), à Hué (capitale de l'ancien Annam) à Haïphong, le port bien connu qui est situé à l'entrée de la célèbre baie d'Along parsemée de rochers fantastiques...

N B. — From Saigon, to Tourane, (marble grottes), to Hué, the capital of Annam Emperors)...

vegetation grew back after each rainy season. The jungle could be controlled, but not suppressed. Trees were cut down selectively, and the forestry commission replanted where necessary or cleared undergrowth. Ta Prohm was left as it was, and nostalgic tourists could still wander off the main path to see its jungle-shrouded ruins, recapturing some of the feelings experienced in this same place by Mouhot or Pierre Loti or his fellow writer Paul Claudel.

A new map drawn up in 1908 gave the curator a clearer picture of his domain. He could now see how the network of monuments interconnected and how dikes and causeways marked the city's old system of waterways; he could pinpoint unidentified ruins that still needed to be studied and described. Known buildings, too, had to be reevaluated as their reconstruction progressed, modifying their appearance. Fallen masonry was replaced and tottering structures were propped up with concrete posts, but all such modest restorations were deliberately kept to a minimum.

Angkor was not officially opened as a park until 1925, but the routes around the site had already been traced and included both a short and long loop, which took in a number of smaller monuments in addition to the principal ones.

The Curator and Tourists

At the beginning of the 1920s Angkor was discovered by the travel companies. The direct road to Saigon and Phnom Penh was still under construction, but flat-bottomed motorboats could cross the Great Lake even

Although Angkor was a long way from the coast it became a regular stopover for wealthy tourists taking a cruise around the world. They came from Saigon or Bangkok in convoys like this one, photographed in front of the Elephant Terrace and the Terrace of the Leper King at Angkor Thom in 1934.

when the waters were low, facilitating year-round access. Arriving by car opposite the entrance to Angkor Wat, the visitor found a comfortable bungalow waiting and official guides on hand to conduct a tour of the site using a variety of transport options: car, elephant ("two people only in the palanquin"), horse, or the incommodious cart, whose comfort had not improved with the roads.

The tourists were either colonials or, increasingly, globetrotters for whom Angkor had become an obligatory stopover. The curator managed to ignore them most of the time. To gain a mention in his excavation journal one had to engrave one's name on a temple—a specialty of sailors on leave—or steal a piece of sculpture. Surveillance measures were sometimes effective and booty was often retrieved from the hotel rooms of this superior class of vandal, but the number of such thefts grew, particularly from isolated sites. Tighter controls were proposed but were slow to be enacted.

More of an irritant, from the curator's point of view, were those visitors recommended by one of the numerous authorities in the Indochinese hierarchy. The degree of attention they required depended upon the rank of the person referring them, but the curator was at least obliged to show them the sculpture depot, a "house of marvels," as one visitor described it, where items

Marshal Joseph Joffre (opposite above), visited Angkor in 1921. With him at Angkor Wat (below) were King Sisowat, the governor-general of Indochina, the senior French official in Cambodia, and the director of the Ecole Française d'Extrême-Orient. In honor of the marshal's visit all work ceased at the various sites, the temples were cleaned, and a road was even opened to make Preah Khan accessible by car. (The road closed again the next day.)

salvaged during clearing were stored. The place was a complete jumble where shapeless fragments lay next to some of the finest examples of Khmer sculptural art.

The curator also received visitors of the highest rank, such as that of the French military hero Marshal Joffre.

Sensuality, Pineapples, and Curses

The staunchly Catholic writer and diplomat Paul Claudel (1868–1955) stopped off at Angkor in 1912 on his way to Japan and gave an account of his brief visit in his *Journal,* later developing it in *Le Poète et le Vase d'Encens* (The Poet and the Incense Jar). His poetic meditation follows the short route around Angkor, but in reverse, beginning with a brief mention of Banteay Kdei, then describing Ta Prohm, Ta Keo, the Gate of Victory, the Bayon, and finally Angkor Wat, whose five towers Claudel likened to pineapples. Claudel's blasphemous "pineapples" caused even more of a sensation than Loti's reference to the Bayon's towers as pinecones, but for him it was Angkor Wat itself that was a "parade of blasphemy"—a place, as he saw it, imbued with evil. Four years later Claudel was once again in Indochina when he heard of Commaille's murder. The

Below: A Thai prince visiting Angkor Wat; autochrome by Léon Busy, c. 1920.

news reinforced his prejudice: "Angkor," he said, "is one of the most accursed, the most evil places that I know. I came back ill, and the account I had written of my journey was destroyed in a fire."

At the start of the 1920s the Angkor conservation program was already well under way, and research projects were proceeding in earnest. In France, meanwhile, at the Colonial Exposition held in Marseilles in 1922 a virtually life-size reconstruction of Angkor Wat's fourth level gave visitors a much clearer idea of the Khmer monuments than any they might have gained from previous exhibitions.

Waking the Sleeping Beauties

In the 1920s a series of controversies arose regarding the temple of Banteay Srei, which lay in the heart of

Pages 102–3: Paul Claudel's "pineapples" at Angkor Wat, and one of Angkor Thom's gateways, drawn by the animal painter Paul Jouve. Jouve also illustrated Pierre Loti's *Un Pèlerin d'Angkor.*

Left: Cover of the sheet music for the foxtrot "When Bhudda Smiles," 1921. The smile was later described by Paul Mus as "neither happy, nor crazy, nor bitter. Human, friendly, knowing."

Below: Postcard showing the reconstruction of Angkor Wat at the Colonial Exposition in Marseilles in 1922 (used again in Paris in 1931).

the jungle, about twelve miles northeast of Angkor Thom. The first, in 1923, involved a well-known French writer in a highly publicized legal dispute. Then, in 1927, a French art historian overturned accepted theories regarding the history of Angkor Thom, and in 1929 a Dutch archaeologist declared that the curator's methods were out of date and better suited to the year 1880.

Banteay Srei, otherwise known as the Citadel of Women, had escaped the notice of Etienne Aymonier and Lunet de Lajonquière. It was discovered in 1914 by an officer from the Geographical Service, who returned from there with a beautiful sculpture of Shiva and Parvati which he gave to the Phnom Penh museum. Shortly afterward Henri Parmentier visited the site and published an admiring article about it. Angkor still had priority, however, and Banteay Srei, like all the out-of-the-way monuments, was abandoned to its jungle fate.

In the Public Arena: the Malraux Affair

André Malraux (1901–76), a talented young avant-garde French writer and art lover who was also an art dealer on the side (later internationally known as an art critic and French minister of culture), read Parmentier's article about Banteay Srei. Having first checked that there were no laws protecting the temple ruins, Malraux then obtained permission to carry out, at his own expense, an archaeological survey of the route linking Thailand with Angkor, and in October 1923 he and his young wife set sail from Marseilles on the *Angkor*.

They visited Angkor with a friend, then all three traveled by cart to Banteay Srei, where they removed several pieces of sculpture forming one of the female figures after which the temple is named. On arriving at Phnom Penh they were arrested and charged with trafficking in antiquities, but not jailed. Six months later they were tried, and the two men received prison sentences. Clara Malraux returned to France to alert her husband's literary friends, and Malraux and his companion were released with suspended sentences following an appeal. The sculptures reverted to the state. Malraux went back to France for a few weeks, then

André Malraux in 1923. The Malraux affair was in every way a triumph of bad faith. On the one hand there was the coolly calculating art lover—whose taste Henri Parmentier, witness for the prosecution, had to admire—and on the other a colonial society for whom what was on trial was the literary avant-garde. In Paris it provoked both venomous articles and supportive petitions from scholars and writers. In the midst of all this the Ecole Française d'Extrême-Orient saw an opportunity to strike an effective blow against looting and looked forward to a more stringent application of the laws protecting temples.

ANDRÉ MALRAUX

LA VOIE ROYALE

ROMAN

UN ROMAN D'AVENTURES PAR

L'AUTEUR DES CONQUÉRANTS

ÉDITIONS BERNARD GRASSET
I Volume 15 fr.

returned to Indochina, where he launched a political attack against colonial exploitation. In 1930 he published *La Voie Royale* (The Royal Way), a romanticized version of his expedition, which Clara later recounted in her memoirs.

One other book came out of the affair, a lavish 1925 publication devoted to Banteay Srei by the Ecole Française d'Extrême-Orient. Goloubew, a lover of fine books, was in charge of the project and wrote about the iconography; splendid large photographs showed the temple that had been so much in the news. Louis Finot dealt with the temple inscriptions, and Parmentier the architecture. A few years later the interpretation of the inscriptions and the proposed reconstruction of the structure both turned out to need some revision.

In Scholarly Circles: Questions Raised by an Art Historian in Paris

The study of Khmer art tended from the outset to be strictly compartmentalized. Different disciplines each had their own separate agenda: Epigraphists determined dates, and archaeologists accepted their findings, even if this meant abandoning their own "artistic intuitions."

Banteay Srei is a case in point. We now know that it was founded in the year 967, but certain decorative details are archaic in character. Parmentier was not far wrong, therefore, when in first publishing it he attributed it to the beginning of the 10th century, linking it with monuments at Roluos, near Angkor, which were securely dated to the very end of the 9th century. In the 1925 publication, however, Finot interpreted the inscriptions in such a way that the temple had to date from the 14th century: Instead of being one of the jewels

Left: Malraux's *La Voie Royale* was promoted not with an image from Banteay Srei but with the more famous smile of the Bayon.

Below: Paul Mus (left) and George Coedès. Coedès published eight volumes of Cambodian inscriptions.

Opposite left: Henri Marchal in 1937. Marchal, who arrived in Cambodia in 1906 and died at Siem Reap in 1970, was responsible for the first successful re-erection of a monument. Behind him is an extract from his highly informative excavation journal.

Opposite right: Louis Finot, in front of one of the Bayon's towers in 1924. He proved that the Bayon was a Buddhist monument.

of Angkor's early art, it became one of its last strokes of genius.

In 1929 George Coedès finally set the record straight. Two years earlier Philippe Stern, in his *Le Bayon d'Angkor et l'Evolution de l'Art Khmer* (The Bayon

at Angkor and the Evolution of Khmer Art), called into
question the entire chronology of Khmer
art and the methods hitherto used to
establish it. "This evolution…should
emerge spontaneously from the
detailed study of the works
themselves," he wrote in 1927
in explanation of his method.
"Only afterward, when conclusions
have been drawn, can they be
compared with those reached by
other disciplines on the same subject."
By "other disciplines" he meant above
all epigraphy. In the light of Stern's
comments Coedès re-examined
the whole body of existing work on

Angkor's inscriptions and concluded that the Bayon was
built by Jayavarman VII, the sovereign responsible for
rebuilding Angkor at the end of the 12th century.

An important point had been established. From now
on art historians and epigraphers pooled their efforts and
in a few years were able to produce definitive dates for
Angkor's history and monuments.

Between Neighbors: A Dutchman in Angkor

The Angkor Conservation Service was modeled to some
extent on the remarkably efficient Archaeological Service
of the Dutch East Indies, whose director, Dr. P. V. van
Stein Callenfels, was invited to Angkor in 1929. Henri
Marchal (1876–1970), curator at the time, showed him
around the sites where restoration work was in progress,
noting in his excavation journal that evening, "He
sharply criticized our working methods and the fact that
when we clear a site we fail to reinstate the fallen
masonry," and acknowledging a case for imitating some
of the procedures practiced by the Dutch.

Marchal was sent to Indonesia, and on his return the
Conservation Service decided to rebuild Banteay Srei. It
was the first total reconstruction project, and the choice
fell on Banteay Srei both because of its artistic interest
and because of the certainty of finding virtually all its
stones in the vicinity—or, in the case of Malraux's stolen

pieces, retrieving them from the Phnom Penh museum.

For the workers employed by the Conservation Service, as for Marchal himself, this was a complete departure from their normal working methods: They were no longer just freeing Angkor from the jungle—they were building it. The operation was a success, and Banteay Srei became one of Angkor's greatest attractions. It also had its educational side, since the rebuilt monument showed that Parmentier's reconstruction drawing had not been entirely accurate.

The Cosmic City

A decade of crises was over, and Angkor Wat regained its dignity. It was once more the centerpiece at the Colonial Exposition, held this time in Paris in 1931. In Cambodia

Opposite: Dr. van Stein Callenfels (center) visiting the Angkor Thom sculpture depot. He introduced Marchal to the technique of anastylosis, which involved dismantling and then rebuilding an existing structure, filling in missing sections with clearly marked new work.

Below: Reconstruction in progress at Banteay Srei, c. 1930.

itself, flying over Angkor, Goloubew finally discovered the true site of the early city built by Yashovarman; the "Central Mountain" turned out to be a natural hill, a "phnom," Phnom Bakheng, crowned by a pyramid bristling with towers.

The Bayon, with its mysterious face-towers, was a continuing source of fascination. In 1933 a young curator called Georges Trouvé discovered a well under its central tower. In it he found the battered remains—buried there by 13th-century iconoclasts —of the giant Buddha erected by Jayavarman VII. The

The international Colonial Exposition, held in Paris in 1931, was inaugurated by Marshal Louis Lyautey and President Gaston Doumergue, seen in the leading car passing the reconstruction of Angkor Wat.

statue was repaired and in 1935 King Monivong presided over a ceremony in which it was restored to its rightful place.

Like the other temple-mountains, the Bayon served as a tomb for its founder, Jayavarman VII, but its significance was also symbolic. In illustration of the Hindu myth of the Churning of the Ocean of Milk, it was the pivot of the churn powered by the giants with serpents in their grip who flank the entrance to Angkor Thom. And it represented the center of the universe, ringed first by mountains (the city walls) and then by the ocean (the surrounding moat). Looking further, the scholar Paul Mus, basing his argument on Cambodian inscriptions and Indian traditions, argued persuasively that the ocean-moat was not in fact impassable: He saw the serpents the giants hold also as rainbows connecting the world of humans to that of the gods.

The Exposition was an opportunity for advertisers to cash in on Angkor. This poster advertising a luxurious Lincoln (above) compares the car, requiring 6500 separate operations in its manufacture, to "those Asian temples, the beauty of whose every detail contributes to the harmony of the whole, produced by generations of craftsmen." In another advertisement one read, "Angkor defies the centuries, the Rolls watch counts them."

During the two years he spent in Indochina on the eve of World War II Jean Despujols (1886–1965) produced three hundred enormously varied paintings and drawings. At Angkor he worked in the same picturesque tradition as Delaporte. The older artist enlivened his Bayon view with a tiger; in *The Temple in the Jungle* Despujols shows one prowling in front of Ta Prohm's famous kapok trees.

Conservation work continued at Angkor throughout the war, despite the devastations of 1945. In 1949 Cambodia achieved self-government as a member of the French Union and in 1953 gained full independence. For the newly independent state, Angkor was more than ever a symbol of its national splendor.

CHAPTER VI

ANGKOR, THE GLORY OF A NATION

For outsiders, Angkor is a dream of ruins in the jungle, such as Ta Prohm (opposite), in 1968. For Cambodians, Angkor Wat is the symbol of nationhood (right).

Toward a Resurrection: Major Measures for Major Projects

The Angkor Conservation Service was managed by the Ecole Française d'Extrême-Orient until Khmer archaeologists could take over. Thanks to Franco-Khmer collaboration it found itself with an unusually large amount of funds, which meant that Angkor, the largest archaeological site in the world, now had the resources to equal its status. The architect J.-P. Laur, and especially the archaeologist who succeeded him in 1960, Bernard-Philippe Groslier (1926–86)—son of George Groslier, founder of the School of Cambodian Arts—were backed by an increasingly large team of specialists and technicians. Their numbers were gradually swelled by young students who came from the school of archaeology at Phnom Penh to acquire practical training at Angkor.

This injection of new resources meant that archaeological work could be undertaken at Angkor on a totally different scale. At Prasat Kravan, for example, Groslier set about restoring the brick towers decorated with reliefs on their inside walls, an operation that required the manufacture of bricks of a special size to match the originals. The project, the first of its kind, was a complete success, both technically and artistically. The Baphuon, on the other hand, was a more typical case. Despite repeated attempts to shore it up, since the 1920s sections of the temple-mountain, Chou Ta-kuan's "bronze tower," kept collapsing. Groslier decided to tackle the problem at its root and had the monument rebuilt around a framework of reinforced concrete—a solution he regarded as "surgery," to be used only as a last resort. It was to serve for the largest projects at Angkor, culminating in Angkor Wat.

The New History

Up to this point excavations had all been localized affairs.

Only with the help of a whole arsenal of modern equipment—cranes and mechanical diggers, as well as new instruments for photographing, surveying, and restoring objects, and for diagnosing causes of deterioration in stone—could a complete restoration of Angkor Wat be undertaken. Below and opposite above: Work in progress in 1968. When the gallery vault was removed above the great relief of the Churning of the Ocean of Milk, temporary thatched roofs were erected to protect the sculptures (to the left of the crane). Opposite below: Blocks of stone at the Baphuon, organized into groups and ready to be replaced in their original positions when the monument is reconstructed. A number of the blocks come from the dismantling of the giant recumbent Buddha that worshipers in the 16th century added to the pyramid's western facade.

Overleaf: A tower of the Bayon (left). Axonometric drawing of the Bayon by Jacques Dumarçay (right). Bernard-Philippe Groslier put into motion the preparation of architectural surveys of all the monuments in the Angkor group. Most have now been published, including Dumarçay's of the Bayon (1967), Ta Keo (1971), and Phnom Bakheng (1972), and Guy Nafilyan's survey of Angkor Wat (1969). Dumarçay recently published a partial survey of a few other monuments on which work had to stop in 1970.

Groslier was a professional archaeologist, familiar with modern techniques, and the scope of his investigations prior to his appointment as curator was much wider, in particular at the royal palace and in the vicinity of Sras Srang. He was interested not just in monuments but in human history. The new topographical survey enabled him to establish the city's system of waterways in its various stages, and the chronology of the buildings emerged from revised imaging of the temples and from accompanying studies. Sculptures, bronzes, and pottery collected since the beginning of the century and duly conserved, photographed, and described helped to complete the picture.

Angkor was not the only focus of attention. Work was also carried out on the temples of the Battambang region to the west, and to the east Beng Mealea, the Great Preah Khan, and the temples strung out along the road linking the two. Excavations were also begun at Sambor Prei Kuk, and the great Kompong Kdei bridge on the road to Kompong Thom was restored and henceforth used by traffic heading for Angkor—just as in Jayavarman VII's time.

Archaeological investigations begun in the 1960s were frequently halted by the disturbances that followed the deposition of Prince Norodom Sihanouk in 1970, after his failure to negotiate the withdrawal of North Vietnamese forces from Cambodian territory. Some publications still appeared, including major sequences of new illustrations; but only one of Groslier's excavation reports has been published to date, that on Sras Srang (in 1988). Work also went on outside the Conservation Service: In 1965 Philippe Stern produced a new study on the monuments contemporary with the Bayon, and in 1966 Jean Boisselier's long-awaited manual on Cambodian archaeology appeared.

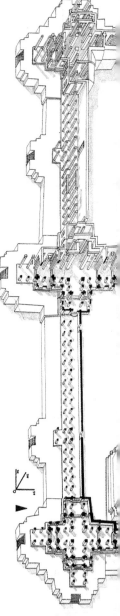

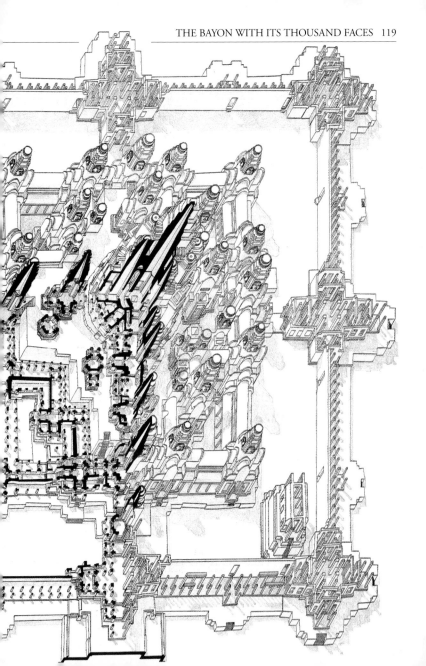

The carvings at Kbal Spean were made in the living rock, and there is no evidence that a permanent building ever existed on the site. The hill represents the Himalayas, the abode of the gods (sculpted in the rock), and the river is the Ganges, which flows down to the Great City, the abode of the Khmer kings.

The Last Explorer

Jean Boulbet was an ethnologist from the Ecole Française d'Extrême-Orient who had taken up residence in Phnom Kulen. He had always been a great walker, and his friends from the village would escort him on hikes through the jungle to show him the "marvels" around which they had built up their history. One day a man known as the "long-haired master," a famous hermit, directed them upriver to an "interesting place" where "the rocks are beautiful and there are ancient engravings on the stone, including a frog, a bull, and various letters."

The place was in fact much more extraordinary than Boulbet and his friends had been led to believe. At the point the hermit had indicated, the river was broken by a series of waterfalls and spanned by a rock bridge, which gave the place its name, Kbal Spean ("bridgehead"). The bed of the river itself was covered with sculptures—frogs and bulls, but also countless *lingams* (phallic shapes emblematic of the god Shiva) and images of Vishnu asleep on his snake, all washed over by the river and rippling with reflected light. One of the sculptures showed a god standing under a portico bearing a large stone lizard; alongside it were the inscriptions mentioned by the hermit.

The "River of a Thousand Lingams" proved to be one of the two upper branches of the main river whose waters, domesticated and channeled, flow down to irrigate Angkor.

The Prince and His Friends

For Prince Norodom Sihanouk visits from foreign heads of state had served as a guarantee of continuing peace in Cambodia. A tour to Angkor would inevitably remind them how much more was at stake in this country than merely the peace and tranquillity of a pleasant life.

President Charles de Gaulle's visit in 1966 culminated in the most glorious celebrations, following his momentous "Phnom Penh address" delivered to the crowd in the city's Olympic stadium.

Festivals at Angkor

When Banteay Srei celebrated its millennium in 1967 the jungle still encroached upon it from all sides, but thanks to a new road the temple was now barely a twenty-minute drive

French President Charles de Gaulle addressed the crowd in the Olympic stadium at Phnom Penh in August 1966 (above). On the same visit, celebrations were held at Angkor Wat (below).

from Angkor, and crowds of tourists flocked to join in the festivities.

Another more official and deeply symbolic festival was held at Angkor Thom, returning the city for a time to its ancient status as capital of the kingdom of Cambodia. In the royal square the "sacred furrow" was drawn to symbolize the first plowing, and at the end of the ceremony the oxen that pulled the "August Plow" were directed toward a series of silver platters, each containing something different—grains of one sort or another, fresh-cut grass, water, or alcohol. Depending on what the animals select to eat, it is thought that a harvest will be good, that the herds will sicken or heavy rains fall, that times of peace or a period of misfortune await. In 1967 a good rice harvest was forecast, and the announcement was greeted with applause.

When a holy man is cremated in Cambodia, the ceremony is another occasion for festivities. A temporary building of bamboo—a *men*, representing Mount Meru—is erected to house the pyre. In the late 1960s, when the head of one of the Siem Reap monasteries died, the *men* was made by workers of the Conservation Service in their spare time. Though less faithful architecturally to its real-life patterns than were the models at the expositions in Marseilles or Paris, it was much more vital, its white paper walls painted with "reliefs" showing the monkey god Hanuman and other deities.

Below: Khmer painting of the monkey god Hanuman building a bridge across the ocean.

The City of the Stars

Angkor has been a magnet for filmmakers, its temples serving as a backdrop for features such as *Lord Jim* and for various episodes in the many films made by Norodom Sihanouk himself. On occasion the prince acted in his own productions, for example in *Ombre sur Angkor* (Shadow over Angkor) which tells of one of the bloody

Every April at the Cambodian new year festival, Chaul Chnam, Cambodians flock in thousands to Angkor Wat, whose galleries are overrun for a few days with people eating, sleeping, playing games. These women ate mangoes on the Angkor Wat causeway in 1968.

Khmer dancers at Angkor Wat, 1969.

episodes that devastated the province of Siem Reap in the 1950s. On another occasion a battle scene at the foot of Angkor Wat set an army of Angkorian soldiers amid charging war elephants. The filming attracted crowds, partly to watch the prince and partly because people enjoyed seeing Angkor brought to life again. The Khmer temples in *Apocalypse Now*, however, filmed in 1979, were of papier mâché and not even made in Cambodia.

The Price of Success

Western interest in Angkor was a mixed blessing: While the arrival of tourists has boosted its economy, it also multiplied the number of collectors. Looting, an endemic problem, was on the increase, not only in isolated temples, but also at more crowded sites with stricter surveillance. One night the animal head of one of Banteay Srei's hybrid guardians disappeared. On another occasion the Leper King's head was attacked with a saw. There was only one answer to the problem: The statues had to be removed from their original setting and housed

The mystery of Angkor was combined with Cold War drama in Bill S. Ballinger's *The Spy at Angkor Wat* (1966).

Below left: One of Prince Norodom Sihanouk's films being shot at Angkor Wat.

Opposite: Statues in the Conservation Service depot, c. 1980. The head of the right-hand figure was chiseled off in 1969 but was recovered as the thieves tried to smuggle it out of the country.

in the sculpture depot. Models were made to replace some of the originals, but many of the pedestals and niches remained bare.

The shadow of a soldier on a bas-relief at Angkor Wat, photographed c. 1980.

April 1970: The Entire Population of Siem Reap Followed Henri Marchal's Funeral Procession

By June 1970 the town was reeling from the effects of war. The Conservation Service, whose headquarters were located just outside Siem Reap, sent its most valuable collections to Phnom Penh to be housed in the museum's vaults. Items that were too heavy to load into a plane remained where they were, protected with sandbags and concrete shields.
The line of fire lay between Siem Reap and Angkor Wat, but restoration work continued on either side of it for another two years. Almost three thousand people from villages to the north had fled for safety to Angkor Wat, among them many of Angkor's workers. Each morning a procession of cyclists made its way from Angkor to the Conservation Service's headquarters and set off again across the line of fire loaded down with supplies including sacks of cement, reinforcing rods, and fuel for the cranes. And equally

regularly, twice a week, Groslier and Boulbet, also on bicycles, came across from their side to inspect the work and bring the men their salaries, which the Phnom Penh government (completely aware of the situation) continued to pay on time. In the middle of a war, both sides deemed that Angkor had to be preserved, and those who looked after it deemed it quite natural to go on working.

This situation was too good to last, and two years later work had to stop. The Baphuon was properly protected, but time ran out before Angkor Wat was secured, and the gallery containing the relief of the Churning of the Ocean of Milk suffered during the ensuing years of neglect. In the 1980s the division of Cambodia hindered national and international efforts to resume the vast task of conservation.

But then in 1994, in his very first decree, the prince who had now become king of a united country laid down rules to protect Angkor from insensitive restoration and commercial pressures. Now, Cambodia, a sovereign state, pools its efforts with those of the international community to insure the survival of what has been a World Heritage Site since 1992.

Sweeper on the Angkor Wat causeway, c. 1980. Day after day, generation after generation, these sweepers attending to the practical upkeep of the temple—sometimes in ones and twos, sometimes in gangs—are a symbol of its endurance through all the vicissitudes of Cambodia's history.

Overleaf: The Bayon, photographed and drawn.

DOCUMENTS

Angkor through the eyes
of those who visited,
interpreted, and reconstructed it

The Journey to Angkor

Angkor offered something completely new even to the most world-weary traveler. In their efforts to understand it, visitors revealed something of themselves.

A Chinese Observer

Chou Ta-kuan arrived at Angkor with an embassy from the Emperor of China in August 1296 and remained there until July 1297.

On the Value of His Work
Inevitably I could not learn about the country and its customs in every detail, but I was nevertheless in a position to establish the principal points....

Cambodia
I imagine it is these monuments [the temples] that account for the glowing reports which foreign merchants have always given of rich and noble Cambodia....
    Each village has either a temple or a tower.... On the main roads are resting places similar to our post houses.

The King of Cambodia
Although they are Barbarians, these people nevertheless know what a prince is....
    Only the prince may wear clothes patterned all over with leaves. He wears a golden diadem.... Instead of the diadem sometimes he simply winds around his head a garland of scented flowers not unlike jasmine. Around his neck he wears about three pounds of large pearls and around his wrists, ankles and arms gold bracelets and rings all set with tiger's eyes. The soles of his feet and the palms of his hands are dyed red.... Whenever he goes out he carries a golden sword in his hand.

One of the "stone generals" flanking the southern causeway of Angkor Thom (left).

The Simplicity of the Cambodian People
In general these people are extremely simple. Whenever they meet a Chinese man they are very shy and respectful and call him "Buddha." As soon as they see him they throw themselves face down on the ground. For some time now there have also been people who cheat and mistreat the Chinese. This is because of the great number now in their country.

All of them, men and women—and this applies to the king too—wear their hair in a chignon and go about with their shoulders bare. They simply wrap a piece of cloth around their loins. When they go out they wrap another, larger piece of cloth round the first....

When they have been to the toilet they always wash themselves in the pool, using their left hand only, since they eat with their right hand. When they see a Chinese person going to the toilet they jeer at him and make as if to prevent him stepping past them.

The Chinese in Cambodia
Chinese sailors who come to this country like not having to wear clothes here, and since, moreover, it is easy to earn enough money to buy rice, and easy to obtain women, equip a house and do business, there are always some who desert in order to [stay] here....

A Chinese always takes a wife as soon as he arrives, deriving additional benefit from the woman's business skills.

Description of the City: The Walls and the Gates
The city walls are approximately twenty furlongs [2.5 miles] in circumference. They have five gateways and each gate is a double one. There are two gates to the east; the other sides have only one gate

each. On the outer side of the wall is a great moat and beyond the moat is a series of large bridges spanning the access moats. On either side of the bridges are fifty-four stone gods like "stone generals"; they are gigantic and terrible to look at....

The five gates are all the same. The parapets of the bridges are made entirely of stone, carved in the shape of serpents with nine heads. The fifty-four deities all hold on to the serpent as if to prevent it from escaping....

Above each gate in the wall there are five great stone Buddha heads, their faces turned towards the cardinal points; the fifth head, in the center, is decorated with gold....

The walls are made entirely of blocks of stone placed one on top of another and rising up to a height of approximately two fathoms [12 feet]. There are no crenellations. Here and there along the rampart *kouang-lang* trees [sago palms] have been planted. There are empty chambers at intervals along the walls. The inner side of the wall is like a glacis more than ten fathoms [60 feet] wide. The large gates at the top of each glacis are shut at night and opened again in the morning, and each gateway has its guardian. Anyone can go through these gates, which are barred only to dogs. The walls form a regular square, on each side of which is a stone tower. Criminals who have had their toes cut off are also forbidden to pass through the gates.

The Interior of the City
At the center of the kingdom is a golden tower [the Bayon] flanked by more than twenty stone towers and several hundred stone chambers. Toward the east is a golden bridge. Placed to the left

Neak Pean, Chou Ta-kuan's "golden tower" in the "Northern Lake": A temple on a circular island, set in a square pool—here dry—in the Preah Khan Baray.

and right of the bridge are two golden lions and at the foot of the stone chambers are eight gold Buddhas....

Approximately one furlong [about 220 yards] to the north of the Golden Tower is a bronze tower [the Baphuon], which is even taller than the Golden Tower and of most impressive appearance. At the foot of the Bronze Tower there are again more than ten stone chambers....

Roughly another furlong to the north [of the Baphuon] lies the king's residence. In the apartments where he rests there is another golden tower [the Phimeanakas?].

The Royal Palace

The royal palace, the official buildings and the residences of the nobility all face east.... The tiles of the principal apartment are made of lead.... The long verandas and covered corridors stretch out and interconnect in a not inharmonious way. The king settles his affairs at a golden window.... I have heard it said that the palace contains many marvels, but the defenses are very secure and I have not been able to see them.

Each time that I did go into the palace to see the king the latter always came out with his first wife and sat at the golden window of the principal apartment.

As regards the Golden Tower inside the palace, it is here, right at the top, that the king goes to sleep at night....

Opposite the royal palace there are twelve small stone towers [the Prasat Suor Prat or Towers of the Rope Dancers]....

The residences of the princes and important officials are built quite differently from those of the people.... The common people would not dare to put the smallest piece of tile on their houses, but cover them instead with thatch.

The Area Around the City
The stone tower [Baksei Chamkrong?] is half a furlong beyond the southern gate. It is said that Lu Pan [a legendary Chinese architect] erected it in a single night. The tomb of Lu Pan [Angkor Wat] is approximately one furlong beyond the southern gate and measures some ten furlongs in circumference. It contains several hundred stone chambers....

The Eastern Lake [Chou Ta-kuan is in fact referring to the Western Baray] is roughly ten furlongs to the east of the walled city and measures some hundred furlongs in circumference. In the center are a stone tower and a number of stone chambers. Inside the tower is a recumbent bronze Buddha from whose navel a constant stream of water flows....

The Northern Lake [Preah Khan Baray] is five furlongs [1100 yards] to the north of the walled city. In the

center is a golden tower of square construction [Neak Pean] together with several dozen stone chambers. As regards the golden lion, golden Buddha, bronze elephant, bronze bull, bronze horse, they are all to be found there....

Festivals in the Royal Square
These people always celebrate the tenth moon.... In front of the royal palace they erect a large platform with room for more than a thousand people and decorate it all over with lanterns and flowers. Opposite, at a distance of twenty fathoms [120 feet]...they erect a high platform.... On the top of this rockets and firecrackers are placed. The costs are borne by the provinces and by the nobility. At nightfall the king is invited to the festivities. The rockets are set off and the firecrackers lit. The rockets can be seen from more than a hundred furlongs [12.5 miles] away, while the firecrackers are as big as mortars and their explosion shakes the whole city. Mandarins and noblemen contribute candles and areca palm wood. The expense is considerable. The king also invites foreign ambassadors to the celebrations.

Chou Ta-kuan
Memorials on the Customs of Cambodia
c. 1297

A Portuguese Traveler at Angkor Wat

The description of Angkor by Diogo do Couto (1543–1616), official chronicler of the Portuguese Indies at the beginning of the 17th century, is based on the observations of a Capuchin friar who visited Angkor in around 1585–8. Omitted from the 1614 publication in which it should have appeared, this account was discovered by Charles Ralph Boxer in 1954 and published in Portuguese, with a French translation, in Angkor et le Cambodge au XVIe Siècle d'Après les Sources Portugaises et Espagnoles *(Paris, 1958).*

Half a league from this city [Angkor Thom] is a temple named Angar [Angkor Wat], which is built on beautiful, flat and open terrain. This temple is a hundred and sixty paces long and so strangely constructed that it cannot be described in writing any more than it can be compared to any other existing monument. The central body of the building comprises four naves

and their vaults rise up, heavily decorated, to form lofty, pointed domes supported by numerous columns worked with all the intricacy of which the human genius is capable. [The temple] is built on a magnificent platform of massive slabs of the same stone as the rest of the edifice. This platform is ascended via a series of admirably cut and remarkable steps flanking it on all sides. At each corner of this large principal structure are smaller temples which correspond in style to the main building, all of them terminating

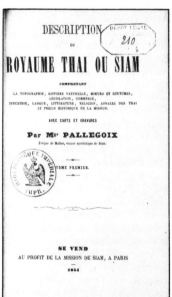

Left: Angkor is absent from 17th- and 18th-century maps, such as that in Simon De La Loubère's work of 1691; it is located to the right of the words "Bas Siam." Below: Title page of Mgr. Pallegoix's book.

in sharply pointed domes whose upper sections are entirely covered in gold. These pointed towers with their globes and banners can be seen from more than four leagues [about 14 miles] away. The temple is surrounded by a moat a musket's shot wide and seven fathoms [42 feet] deep, which is spanned by a bridge corresponding to the only gate into the central courtyard. At the entrance (to this bridge) are two stone tigers, one on either side, so massive and terrifying in appearance that they frighten all who enter there. The whole bridge is covered with arches delicately sculpted in freestone and presenting a most noteworthy sight. The temple is surrounded by numerous smaller buildings of great beauty, and the pillars supporting the galleries, like the window posts, [are] made of the same stone and so highly polished that they look as if they had been turned on a lathe.

Diogo do Couto,
in *Angkor et le Cambodge au XVIe Siècle d'Après les Sources Portugaises et Espagnoles* (Angkor and Cambodia in the 16th Century According to Portuguese and Spanish Sources), early 17th century

A Missionary Who Did Not Visit Angkor

It is near the banks of this lake [the Great Lake] that the marvelous ruins of Nokorvat are situated. They consist of a vast palace, columns, pyramids, and temples or pagodas, all in chiseled marble. Of note are the domes and vaulted ceilings whose workmanship is so astonishing that the Cambodians themselves always refer to them as the work of angels rather than men. These ruins probably date from the time of the famous king of Cambodia Phra-Pathum-Surivong, during whose reign a talapoin [monk] from Ceylon came bearing Buddhist texts and introduced Cambodia to the religion of the Buddha.

Mgr. Jean-Baptiste Pallegoix,
Description du Royaume Thai ou Siam (Description of the Thai Kingdom or Siam), 1854

And One Who Did

Charles-Emile Bouillevaux visited Angkor briefly in December 1850, in the course of years spent as a missionary in Indochina. An account of his visit (the first version is below) appeared in Paris in 1858. He was in France in 1865–7 and returned for good in 1873. In 1874 he published L'Annam et le Cambodge, in which his description of Angkor was expanded and accompanied by a diatribe on the "discovery" of the site.

In order to appreciate the splendors of the ancient civilization of Cambodia one must go to Angkor, which lies beyond the great lake, a little over two days' journey from Battambang. Only there is it possible to gain a true impression of what the Maha Nokor Khmer was once like. In our own century the Orient no longer counts: It has grown soft and self-indulgent. The Orient of antiquity, on the other hand, is the strange and wonderful realm of priestly mysteries and gigantic ruins.

After leaving the modern city of Angkor I walked for more than a league over burning sand, which sorely afflicted my poor bare feet. Then suddenly, on leaving the forest, I found I was standing near a wide freestone causeway whose entrance was guarded by fantastic lions. The causeway crosses a pond, where a herd of buffalos were wallowing

Statue of Vishnu worshiped at Angkor Wat.

and feeding. Following it, I saw here and there a number of small semi-derelict pavilions whose former elegance was still apparent despite their ruinous condition. Further on I passed beneath two rather narrow rectangular galleries, whose walls were covered with sculptures, before arriving in front of the pagoda proper.

The Angkor pagoda, which is fairly well preserved, is the jewel of the Indochinese peninsula and worthy of ranking alongside our most beautiful monuments. There is no resemblance between this Buddhist temple and a European church. The main body of the building forms a perfect square; at each corner there is a beautiful tower that ends in a dome and, in the center, a fifth tower looms over the rest. All these towers are linked by great galleries whose walls are decorated with sculptures. One would have to be an artist, however, to give an exact picture of the Angkor pagoda, which is in a style of architecture all its own. Despite its strangeness I found it imposing, magnificent.

I have already mentioned that public instruction, in other words, preaching, did not exist among the worshipers of Sommocudom: A pagoda was not, therefore, a place where worshipers come to be taught. It appears that the Angkor pagoda was built to hold the sacred books brought from Ceylon. Beneath the central tower is a very ordinary statue of the Buddha, said to have been presented by the king of Thailand. The Cambodians also worship a number of other statues of Indian divinities, all of which have sustained some damage. On feast days the wretched idolaters come and prostrate themselves before all these monsters and burn perfumed matches at their feet while the bonzes [Buddhist monks] chant prayers in Pali.

These pagan priests no longer live in the galleries of the old temple but in miserable huts made of wood and straw alongside the glorious monument which their forefathers erected. While I was admiring these remains of Cambodia's former splendor the bonzes, summoned by the gong and the tom-tom, went off to recite in Pali prayers they could not even understand.

When I had visited the pagoda I made my way toward the old city, where the Cambodian kings once resided. I soon crossed the ramparts, which are still standing, and entered the enclosure through a fairly well-preserved gateway. Approximately half a league from the outer wall I came across some vast ruins, which I was told belonged to the royal palace. In architectural style this resembled the pagoda. Among the sculptures smothering the walls I saw elephants fighting and men attacking one another with clubs and lances or drawing back their bows and releasing three arrows at once. These were not the only ruins: There are ruins everywhere inside the old city. Everything I saw at Angkor proves to me unequivocally that Cambodia was once rich, civilized and much more heavily populated than it now is; but all these riches have disappeared and the civilization has died out. Within the walls of the old capital a dense forest now grows and giant trees have taken root in the midst of ruined palaces. There are few things that can stir such melancholy feelings as the sight of places that were once the scene of some glorious or pleasurable event, but which are now deserted.

Charles-Emile Bouillevaux
Voyage dans l'Indo-Chine 1848–1856, 1858

The "Official" Discoverer

News of Henri Mouhot's early death in Laos in 1861 did not reach his friends until the following spring. Britain had been his home since 1856, and The Illustrated London News, *known for its interest in archaeology and exploration, devoted this obituary to him.*

The long list of martyrs to the cause of science has just received an addition in the person of Henri Mouhot, a naturalist and zoological traveller of no mean acquirements, of untiring industry, and indomitable courage. M. Mouhot was a Frenchman by birth, but, having married into a branch of the family of the late Mungo Park, the African traveller, had become an Englishman in habits, and always gave the scientific societies of this country the benefit of his discoveries. In 1858 he left England for Siam, and, after exploring that country and the adjoining territory of Camboja, was at the time of his death en route for the frontiers of the south-western provinces of China. When far in the interior he was attacked by the fever of the country, and expired after twenty-two days' illness…. At a meeting of the Royal Geographical Society…Sir R. Murchison took the opportunity of some letters being read from M. Mouhot in reference to the topography of Camboja to pay a tribute to the merits of this gentleman as a zoological collector and geographical explorer. His loss will be severely felt by men of science, and it will, perhaps, be long before another adventurer is found hardy enough to follow in his footsteps through the wild and fever-stricken countries, for the exploration of which

Mouhot in the forests of Laos.

he sacrificed his home, his health, and eventually his life.

The Illustrated London News
2 August 1862

Mouhot's findings were published after his death. By the end of 1862 a two-volume work in English was in preparation, dedicated "To the learned societies of England." It was edited by his brother, who explained that it was compiled from Mouhot's private letters, journal, sketches, and drawings, unfinished papers, and a paper "destined for the Archaeological Society of London, on the interesting ruins of Ongcor." A less-scholarly account based on Mouhot's journal was serialized in France in 1863. The English-language work came out in 1864 and is the source of the following extracts.

Nokhor, or Ongcor, was the capital of the ancient kingdom of Cambodia, or Khmer, formerly so famous among the great states of Indo-China, that almost the only tradition preserved in the country mentions that empire as having had twenty kings who paid tribute to it, as having kept up an army of five or six million soldiers, and that the buildings of the royal treasury occupied a space of more than 300 miles [*sic*].

In the province still bearing the name of Ongcor, which is situated eastward of the great lake Touli-Sap, towards the 14th degree of north lat., and 104° long. east of Greenwich, there are, on the banks of the Mekon, and in the ancient kingdom of Tsiampois (Cochin-China), ruins of such grandeur, remains of structures which must have been raised at such an immense cost of labour, that, at the first view, one is filled with profound admiration, and cannot but ask what has become of this powerful race, so civilised, so enlightened, the authors of these gigantic works?

One of these temples—a rival to that of Solomon, and erected by some ancient Michael Angelo—might take an honourable place beside our most beautiful buildings. It is grander than anything left to us by Greece or Rome, and presents a sad contrast to the state of barbarism in which the nation is now plunged.

Unluckily the scourge of war, aided by time, the great destroyer, who respects nothing, and perhaps also by earthquakes, has fallen heavily on the greater part of the other monuments; and the work of destruction and decay continues among those which still remain standing, imposing and majestic, amidst the masses of ruins all around.

One seeks in vain for any historical souvenirs of the many kings who must have succeeded one another on the throne of the powerful empire of Maha-Nocor-Khmer. There exists a tradition of a leprous king, to whom is attributed the commencement of the great temple, but all else is totally forgotten. The inscriptions, with which some of the columns are covered, are illegible; and, if you interrogate the Cambodians as to the founders of Ongcor-Wat, you invariably receive one of these four replies: "It is the work of Pra-Eun, the king of the angels;" "It is the work of the giants;" "It was built by the leprous king;" or else, "It made itself."…

I shall commence with the temple of Ongcor, the most beautiful and best preserved of all the remains, and which is also the first which presents itself to the eye of the traveller, making him forget all the fatigues of the journey, filling him with admiration and delight, such as would be experienced on finding a verdant oasis in the sandy desert. Suddenly, and as if by enchantment, he seems to be transported from barbarism to civilisation, from profound darkness to light....

If, starting from this point, you follow for about a couple of hours in the same direction a dusty sandy path passing through a dense forest of stunted trees; and having also frequently crossed the river, which is exceedingly sinuous in its course, you will arrive at an esplanade about 9 metres wide by 27 long, parallel to the building. At each angle, at the extremity of the two longer sides, are two enormous lions, sculptured out of the rock, and forming, with the pedestals, only a single block. Four large flights of steps lead to the platform.

From the north staircase, which faces the principal entrance, you skirt, in order to reach the latter, a causeway 230 metres in length by 9 in width, covered or paved with large slabs of stone, and supported by walls of great thickness. This causeway crosses a ditch 220 metres wide, which surrounds the building; the revetment, 3 metres high by 1 metre thick, is formed of ferruginous stone, with the exception of the top row, which is of freestone, each block being of the same thickness as the wall. [There follows a detailed description of the elements and sculptures of the temple.]...

What strikes the observer with not less admiration than the grandeur, regularity, and beauty of these majestic buildings, is the immense size and prodigious number of the blocks of

Northern facade of Angkor Wat.

stone of which they are constructed. In this temple alone are as many as 1532 columns. What means of transport, what a multitude of workmen, must this have required, seeing that the mountain out of which the stone was hewn is thirty miles distant!...

A temple, about 100 metres in height, built of limestone has been erected on the top of Mount Bakhêng, which is situated two miles and a half north of Ongcor-Wat, on the road leading to the town. At the foot of the mountain are to be seen, among the trees, two magnificent lions, [2 metres and] 20 centimetres in height, and each formed, with the pedestals, out of a single block. Steps, partly destroyed, lead to the top of the mountain, whence is to be enjoyed a view so beautiful and extensive, that it is not surprising that these people, who have shown so much taste in their buildings, should have chosen it for a site.... All this region is now lonely and deserted as formerly it must have been full of life and cheerfulness; and the howling of wild animals, and the cries of a few birds, alone disturb the solitude. Sad fragility of human things!...

Half-a-mile beyond Bakhêng are the ruins of Ongcor-Thôm. A partly-destroyed road, hidden by thick layers of sand and dust, and crossing a large ditch, half filled with blocks of stone, portions of columns, and fragments of sculptured lions and elephants, leads to the gateway of the town, which is built in the style of a triumphal arch.

These remains are in a tolerable state of preservation, and are composed of a central tower, 18 metres high, surrounded by four turrets, and flanked by two other towers connected together by galleries. At the top are four immense

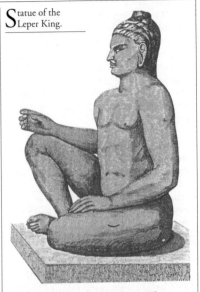

Statue of the Leper King.

heads in the Egyptian style.... The walls, still intact, are covered with bas-reliefs, disposed in four rows, one above another, each representing a king seated in the Oriental fashion, with his hands resting on a broken poignard, and by his side a number of women. All these figures are covered with ornaments, such as very long earrings, necklaces, and bracelets. Their costume is the langouti, and all wear high head-dresses terminating in a point, and apparently composed of precious stones, pearls, and gold and silver ornaments.

On another side the bas-reliefs represent combats; and here are children with long hair tied up like the savages of the East. Everything here, however, yields in beauty to the statue of the leprous king, which is at the end of the terrace. The head, admirable in its nobility, regularity of feature, and gentle yet proud expression, must have been the work of the most skilful sculptor of the country, in an age when many, doubtless, evinced great talent. A small moustache covers his upper lip, and his hair falls in long curls over his shoulders; but the whole body is naked, and without ornament. One foot and one hand are broken....

I have written these few notes on Cambodia, after returning from a long hunting expedition, by the light of a torch, seated on my tiger-skin. On one side of me is the skin of an ape just stripped off; on the other, a box of insects waiting to be arranged and packed; and my employment has not been rendered easier by the sanguinary attacks of mosquitoes and leeches. My desire is, not to impose my opinions on any one, especially with regard to the wonderful architectural remains which I have visited, but simply to disclose the existence of these monuments, which are certainly the most gigantic, and also to my mind display a more perfect taste than any left to us by the ancients; and, moreover, to collect all the facts and traditions possible about these countries, hoping they may be useful to explorers of greater talent and fortune. For, I doubt not, others will follow in my steps, and, aided by their own government and by that of Siam, advantages denied to myself, will gather an abundant harvest where I have but cleared the ground.

Henri Mouhot,
Travels in the Central Parts of Indo-China (Siam), Cambodia and Laos, 1864

A Scholar-Photographer

After a university education in his native Edinburgh, John Thomson took up photography and moved to the Far East

in 1862. He explored Angkor in 1866, the first year of the Doudart de Lagrée mission. His powers of observation and reasoning were acute; his books and the comments he later made at a meeting of the Royal Geographical Society in London (of which he was a Fellow) shed light on some of the practical difficulties of his work.

Many of the ruins are important, and are linked together by stone causeways raised well above the autumn flood levels, and were evidently intended and used by the ancients for extensive traffic from city to city. Adjoining the causeways one finds great stone reservoirs which must have been designed for use during the dry season, when water is scarce.... The quarries from which the stone was obtained are thirty miles distant from Angkor Wat, and one can hardly conceive of any means by which they could have drawn the huge blocks over hilly ground to the capital.... The King of Siam sent a special envoy to request me to photograph the entire series, a request with which I was unable to comply. At the time the kodak was unknown, and one had to depend on the collodion wet plate process of photography. This entailed the constant presence of eight or ten porters to transport the necessary apparatus.

Journal of the Royal Geographical Society, 1893

The Governor had indeed done us the honour to despatch two elephants for our own riding, and five buffalo waggons for our baggage. The elephant howdahs were dome-shaped, of a kind used only by persons of a superior rank.... [The elephant] marches with

The elephants and howdahs used by John Thomson and H. G. Kennedy (of the British Embassy in Bangkok). In the background is the western entrance to Angkor Wat.

Detail of a photograph by Thomson of a face-tower of the Bayon.

a steady step onwards to his destination, knowing, apparently, all about the country. On he goes through pools and marshes, but keeping an eye the while on the spreading branches of the trees above; for somehow, with a marvellous exactness, he knows the howdah's height, and if a branch would barely clear it, he halts, raises his trunk, and wrenches it off before he ventures to proceed....

We spent several days at the ruined city of Nakhon, on the verge of the native jungle, and amidst a forest of magnificent trees. Here we were surrounded on every side by ruins as multitudinous as they were gigantic; one building alone [the Bayon] covered an area of vast extent, and was crowned with fifty-one stone towers. At the outer gate of this city I experienced a sort of modern "battle of the apes." Reared high above the gateway stood a series of subordinate towers, having a single larger one in their centre, whose apex again displayed to us the four benign faces of the ancient god. The image was partly concealed beneath parasitic plants, which twined their clustering fibres in a rude garland around the now neglected head. When I attempted to photograph this object, a tribe of black apes, wearing white beards, came hooting along the branches of the overhanging trees, swinging and shaking the boughs, so as to render my success impossible. A party of French sailors, who were assisting the late Captain de Lagrée in his researches into the Cambodian ruins, came up opportunely, and sent a volley among my mischievous opponents; where-upon they disappeared with what haste they might, and fled away till their monkey jargon was lost in the recesses of the forest.

John Thomson,
The Straits of Malacca, Indo-China and China, 1875

A Meticulous Research Program

Ernest Doudart de Lagrée drew up the following archaeological program for the Mekong Exploration Commission.

Establish the boundaries of former Cambodia according to tradition and the position of the principal ruins.

At Angkor, and anywhere where there are ancient monuments or cities, adopt the following course:

1. Make a general plan of the city and establish which buildings require detailed study.

2. Arrange for all the ancient inscriptions to be copied *without exception,* noting their exact location.

3. Draw plans, sections, and elevations of the principal buildings, recording each building *in the minutest detail.*

4. Where it is not too difficult to do so,

take casts of reliefs. Either by taking a cast or by drawing, put together a collection of types of figures, clothing, weapons, ornaments, etc., as these appear on the reliefs.

5. Make a careful note of any indications regarding the absolute or relative age of each monument.

6. Study general building methods and in particular those employed in the construction of bridges, vaults and roads. Investigate the mechanical methods that may have been employed —how foundations were built—the coloring of buildings—gilding— facing, etc.

7. The distribution of buildings and purpose of their various parts. Investigate remains of private dwellings and, where necessary, excavate.

8. Investigate the provenance of the various construction materials used. If possible, establish the location of the old quarries.

Villemereuil, who edited Doudart de Lagrée's manuscripts, added the following note:

This program seems exhaustive and could, in our opinion, serve as a model for any archaeological investigation. De Lagrée himself appears to have followed it point by point. There is a single omission: "Study the monuments from the religious angle." These words appeared at the end of the program, but were then deleted. Clearly the author felt that neither he nor his companions had the necessary expertise to carry out such a study.

A. de Villemereuil, ed., *Explorations et Missions de Doudart de Lagrée, Extraits de Ses Manuscrits,* 1883

Working at Angkor

November 1901—Letter V—ANGKOR THOM. The journey from Phnom Penh was like a dream. After leaving the *Lutin* we navigated the flooded forest in sampans. In the moonlight, which was magnificent, the woods took on shades of molten silver. And what incredible vegetation emerging from the depths of the water! Every possible shade of green and purple, and every species, too, from the massive banyan to the elegant rustling bamboo. We passed the odd village half hidden beneath areca palms 50 meters tall. Inquisitive women smiled at us as we passed. The huts on stilts were illuminated in honor of the new moon. It was all as bright as daylight and the color was indescribable. Arrival and bed at Siem Reap 11:30. The admiral in a junk. Next day we leave for Angkor in buffalo-drawn carts. What a picture! Thirty-five carts all higgledy-piggledy in the one and only street. Under a beautiful sunrise. We all rush to choose our vehicle and pad it as much as possible: These carts have no springs! But they get about everywhere. We leave in single file. The buffalos trotted—in honor of the admiral, no doubt. Arrival at Angkor Thom. A marvel! Especially the temple of the Baion ("Bayhon" means "king's room" in Cambodian). To get inside you have to cross a wall of enormous fallen stones that shift under your feet and pass through galleries populated by a colony of giant bats which the bonzes have left undisturbed for centuries. The temple is supported by three terraces lying one on top of another and marvelously decorated. There is a fantastic view from the second terrace. And not an inch of stone that isn't

Charles Carpeaux in front of a bas-relief at the Bayon, 1903.

sculpted with unbelievable richness and a charming naiveté of expression. The fifty-two towers, each decorated with four colossal heads of Brahma, are topped with a headdress of vines and even large trees. Angkor Thom is a world in itself. The outer wall is four kilometers [2.5 miles] long on each side. It is impossible to imagine the effect of these Brahma heads worn smooth over the centuries, covered with lichen and shrouded in vines, which the sun's rays still manage to penetrate, playing over these enormous faces and giving each a different expression: some are smiling, others look sad, others impassive…. And the bonzes walk to and fro draped in their yellow togas, sometimes praying in the temple, sometimes cutting wood to cook on. We must have been quite a sight coming down the Angkor Thom steps in our vehicles. The carts bounced like mad! We were like pancakes in a frying pan…. It was hilarious. What somersaults! A ship's captain arrived at the bottom with his legs in the air, and a fat architect started off on his back and arrived on his belly. As for the admiral, he never moved a muscle: He is quite an extraordinary man.

It's a major task shifting those enormous stones that sprawl in the galleries with their gaping roofs and on the crumbling remains of fallen pillars. But they have to be cleared if we want to draw up plans, and the sculpted slabs have to be sorted so we can piece together the reliefs, which record the sacred history of this country. Our coolies are now quite familiar with rollers and inclined planes. But it was worth seeing the look of amazement on these people's faces when they first saw the great stone ceiling slabs sliding 10 meters [about 33 feet] thanks to a small roller we had inserted beneath them. At first the bonzes were anxious about what would happen to their gods, but when they realized nobody was making off with anything they stopped following us everywhere. Extraordinarily enough, one of them even helped us move a large stone at one point when we were having a bit of difficulty. We applauded him, much to his surprise and delight. I am very popular with the bonzes. I successfully treated one who had stomach pains and another who had been bitten by a snake. They keep pressing bananas and fresh coconuts on me.…

6 December 1901. Spent the day at Angkor Thom: obtained the services of several local workmen. Worked on the bas-reliefs at the Baion. They depict religious ceremonies, battles, hunts and, in particular, scenes from the *Mahabharata.* Removed a sculpted stone: two elephants pulling in opposite directions on a rope attached to a statue. Climbed the central tower right up to the Brahma heads at the risk of breaking our necks twenty times over. The interpreter implores us not to leave our *sala* [bamboo hut] in this unwholesome spot. All the nearby huts have been abandoned and several bonzes are laid up, shivering with fever. We've promised him he can sleep at Angkor Wat each night. Been to see the sick bonzes, telling them tomorrow we'll bring them quinine, which will cure them. Been to Siem Reap to exchange correspondence with the School. Killed a magnificent eagle on the way there. On our return impossible to track down the cook, who was presumably playing or smoking opium somewhere. He had to do the journey from Siem Reap on foot with 10 chickens, 5 loaves of bread, and

several dozen eggs on his back.

F. wired us to say he was arriving. He appeared in the early evening accompanied by a friend, a young man who talks a lot about his religion, his poetry and his bathtub. Not a bad chap even so.…

15 April 1904. Went to the Angkor Wat festival for an hour. Monument a strange sight. Hundreds of Cambodian men and women decked out in brightly colored scarves wandering through ruins that are usually deserted. People singing and dancing; in the cruciform gallery they do the stag dance. A man astride a stick with a stag's head at one end complete with horns dances in front of a line of people carrying long, strangely decorated sticks. These people form a tight-knit row and chant very slowly while taking a small step forward, then a small step back. The stag-man is baited by two other men wearing monkey masks whom he charges from time to time.

Charles Carpeaux
Les Ruines d'Angkor, 1908

The Mysterious Sculptures of Angkor Thom

The Bayon Before Rain
Approached through the gloom, the "Victory Gate" looked at first sight like the entrance to a cave. In fact the top of the gate is decorated with monstrous faces of Brahma, but these were hidden from view by the tangle of roots, and on each side, in a kind of niche under the leaves, misshapen three-headed elephants lurk.

We stepped through the gate, crowned with its somber faces, and entered what was once an immense city.…

Unidentifiable fragments of architecture lay in all directions, overrun with ferns, cycads, orchids, all the flora of that eternal twilight filtering through the canopy of tall trees. Numerous Buddhist idols, seated on thrones and ranging in size from the small to the gigantic, smiled at the void....

Palaces once stood here; here kings once lived a life of prodigious luxury—kings of whom we now know nothing, who have sunk into oblivion without leaving so much as a name engraved on a stone or in the memory of men. These tall rocks now blending with the forest, enveloped and clasped by a myriad roots like the tentacles of an octopus, are the work of human hands.

For there is a stubborn will to destruction even in the world of plants. The Prince of Death, whom the Brahmans call Shiva, he who created for each beast that special enemy by which it is devoured, for each creature the gnawing microbes that leach its essence, seems, from the dawn of time, to have foreseen that men would endeavor to prolong their own lives by building things that last. So, to annihilate their work, he thought up, among a thousand other agents of destruction, these plants that grow on walls, and in particular the strangler fig that obliterates everything.

It is this fig tree that is lord of Angkor today. Everywhere, over palaces and over temples, which it patiently breaks apart, it spreads in triumph its pale, smooth branches with their snake-like markings and its broad dome of leaves. It started life as no more than a tiny seed, sown by the wind on a frieze or at the top of a tower. But as soon as it could germinate its roots thrust like delicate filaments between the stones and made their way downward, ever downward, guided by an unerring

instinct, towards the earth and when, at last, they met it they rapidly swelled with life-giving sap until they became enormous, breaking everything apart, destabilizing everything, rending immense walls from top to bottom. From that moment the building was lost, its fate sealed....

Before we knew it there was a drumming on the leaves all around us and rain was falling in sheets! Above the trees the sky had suddenly darkened, but we had failed to notice. The water was streaming down, pouring in torrents on our heads. The only answer was to take refuge by a great dreamy-faced Buddha, in the shelter of his thatched roof.

When the rain finally subsided darkness was falling: It was time we left the jungle if we wished to avoid being caught there at nightfall. But we had almost reached the *Bayon*, Angkor's oldest sanctuary, famous for its *towers with four faces*. Through the trees, now in deep shadow, we caught sight of it from where we stood, looming like a chaotic jumble of rocks. Why not go and see it, we thought.

To reach the temple we had to beat a path with sticks through the tangle of thorn bushes and vines which spread in all directions. The jungle closes in on it from all sides, smothering and crushing it, and giant fig trees complete the work of destruction, taking root everywhere, even on the top of its towers, which serve the trees as pedestals. We had reached the gates. Roots like ancient strands of hair draped them with a thousand fringes, and at this late hour, in the darkness falling from the trees and the rainy sky, they formed deep shadowy holes which we hesitated to step beneath. Sheltering under the

T a Prohm, "clasped by a myriad roots like the tentacles of an octopus."

nearest entrance a group of monkeys were sitting in a circle holding counsel together. At our approach they moved off without a sound—as if silence were a rule of this place. All we could hear was the furtive rustle of drops of water, gathered during the storm, dripping from leaves and stones....

Before leaving, however, I looked up at those towers looming over me, smothered in vegetation, and suddenly I started, overcome with a peculiar kind of fear, on seeing a frozen smile of giant proportions directed down at me... and then I saw another smile, over on another section of wall... and then another three, another five, another ten; they were everywhere, and giant eyes were observing me from all sides.... I had been told about these "towers with four faces," but I had forgotten about them.... The masks sculpted high up there in the air are of such superhuman dimensions that it takes a moment to make them out. Beneath the great flat noses the mouths are smiling, and the eyelids are half closed in a coyly feminine way. They look like old women wearing mildly sardonic expressions, these images of gods worshiped long ago by a people whose history is now lost to us. Over the centuries neither the slow work of the jungle nor the heavy dissolving rains have been able to eradicate that *expression*, that look of ironic benevolence which is even more troubling than the rictus of China's monsters....

The Bayon After Rain

Wherever I look I see those great Brahma faces, the "debonair old ladies," so sly and unnerving the other evening in the dusk, smiling down at me again from among the ferns and roots. There are many more of them than I realized: I can see them even on the most distant towers, wearing crowns on their heads and necklaces at their throats. But in broad daylight they have lost their power to frighten. This morning they seem to say to me: "Look, we are dead and cannot harm you. There is nothing ironic about our smile or our closed eyes; we are smiling like this because we are at peace, sleeping a dreamless sleep."...

The Bayon at Last

In silhouette these squat towers with their row upon row of crowns looked like colossal pine cones pointing at the sky. It was as if stone vegetation had sprung from the ground, thrusting up too thickly, too vigorously. Fifty towers of varying size rose up in tiers, fifty fantastic pinecones bundled together on a base as big as a town, almost jostling one another, clustered like

attendants round a central tower of still greater size, sixty or seventy meters [200–230 feet] high and looming above them, blossoming at its tip into a golden lotus. And from their airy height those four faces on each of the towers looked towards the four cardinal points, looked in all directions, from between the same lowered lids, with the same expression of ironic pity, the same smile. Obsessively, over and over, they affirmed the omnipresence of Angkor's god. Wherever one stood in this vast city one saw those aerial faces, sometimes from the front, sometimes in profile or turned at an angle, sometimes somber when the skies hung low and heavy with rain, sometimes glowing like red-hot iron as a scorching sun fell below the horizon, and on moonlit nights bluish and ghostly, but always there, their presence dominating the city. And yet today their reign is over: you have to look carefully to pick them out from the greenish half-light, and a time will come when they are indistinguishable from their surroundings.

An extraordinary energy has gone into the creation of the many reliefs and the whole array of scrollwork embellishing the Bayon's walls. There are battles, too, furious melees, war chariots, interminable processions of elephants and groups of Apsaras and Tevadas wearing elaborate crowns— all of it gradually disappearing, fading into oblivion, beneath the moss. These sculptures are more childish and primitive in execution than those at Angkor Wat, but also more violent, more passionate in inspiration. And such profusion is disconcerting: In our small-minded age, we can scarcely conceive of the perseverance,

A tower of the Bayon and a gate of Angkor Thom: Illustrations by Paul Jouve from the 1930 edition of Pierre Loti's *Un Pèlerin d'Angkor*.

richness and faith, the love of the grandiose and the eternal, that inspired this lost nation.

Concealed beneath the central tower with its golden lotus, twenty or so meters [about 65 feet] above the plain, lies the Holy of Holies, a dark little recess crammed like a blockhouse into the thickness of the wall. At one time it could be reached from different directions via a network of converging galleries as gloomy as mortuary chambers. But the galleries are now cluttered with fallen masonry, making access to this place both difficult and dangerous. Crouching inside, it is as if one crouched beneath the jungle itself— since the jungle smothers even the towers—beneath the multiple strands of an endless network of roots. It is almost pitch black. Warm water oozes out of the walls and gathers on the few gods that inhabit the place, some armless, some headless, and shadowy as phantoms. Snakes rustle and nameless creatures crawl away in the darkness. Bats woken from sleep protest, approaching on invisible wings to strike the intruder with those rapidly beating membranes. In Brahmanic times men must have trembled in this Holy of Holies, refuge of the ancient mysteries, and even after centuries of neglect the mysteries and the fear persist. Stand still and the furtive inhabitants of the place fall silent too and everything sinks back at once into some indescribable *waiting* horror where the silence weighs too heavy.

Pierre Loti
Un Pèlerin d'Angkor
(An Angkor Pilgrim), 1912

Dancers and the "Devil's Own Temple"

Left for Cambodia by car Sunday 2 October. The great plain flooded. Phnom Penh, M. Baudoin, M. Groslier. The Ecole des Arts with its seemingly telescopic roofs with their multiple setbacks. Visit to King Sisowat. Pagoda paved with silver tiles. Next day left for Angkor at 9 AM on board a M[essageries] boat. Woke next day at 3 AM. View of the enormous river, its great soft muddy waves with carpets of *luk binh* (water hyacinths) floating on them. The flooded forest, then Angkor. Benkhdai, then Ta Prohm buried under vegetation and trees. An atmosphere of fever and decay. Giant white kapok trees digesting the stone embedded in their anastomosis, that root that envelops an entire portico and becomes a pillar itself. The mound of Takeo, whose proportions are in the vertical rather than the horizontal plane. The Angkor Thom bridge, flanked on either side by a balustrade of fifty-four giants, the first with seven heads, hauling the Naga snake. The Bayon with its pylons with four Brahma heads directed toward the four cardinal points. In the afternoon the temple of Angkor Wat, a mass of brown rubble (limonite) covered with gray sandstone, much the same as that at Fontainebleau. In the courtyards, under the lichen, this sandstone takes on silver patterns. Facade with long horizontal, asymmetrical lines, interrupted by a small doorway. This vast temple is reached by a series of cat-flaps, clearly visible, high up, forming a small black hole in the central palace. All around it is a great square lake, then a superimposed series of three other square enclosures surrounded by

galleries connecting midpoint pavilions, the two last with pineapples at each corner. All the pavilions are in the shape of a cross…. In the middle the great central pineapple beneath which stood the image of Shiva, god of love and destruction. Then four other pineapples flanking the central one. In the morning, seen from a distance, they seem to bristle, their uneven outlines creating the effect of wings or flames. A winged egg, a flamboyant jewel. The underlying conception is that of a primeval lake with, in the center, a pavilion rising up like a lotus. Above this first enclosure there is a second (on a plinth which with its broken lines looks like a pile of cushions), then a third, and finally, much higher up, a fourth containing the central Sanctuary. Each of these sanctuaries is in the shape of a cross that is both open and discreetly closed towards the four cardinal points via a portico with three vaults of ever-decreasing height—symbolizing an ascension by a prescribed and concealed path. In effect, a series of lakes (the water damned and stagnant) superimposed as if on trays. Enclosures like entrenchments serving as some kind of defence. The single little black door, the little hole, opening on to a mysterious world, as if framing the night. The plinths as if artificially raised, like a coiled snake. The sanctuaries at the four cardinal points (reminiscent of Cherubims) with the central pylon. Those nocturnal shrines where bats fly in and out (they were flying there already), reeking of a vile, slightly sweet smell (probably emanating from their droppings). Those closed jewels adored from a distance, with the worm at their center, that blasphemous monstrance. Those round boxes, those balls up there in the sky, closed up, full of night and droppings. Had I seen the Devil's own temple, spewed out by the earth? Hence the attackers' extraordinary rage, the fury they unleashed on all the idols, leaving in some cases not a single image, even in pieces, even pulverized. Everywhere those apsaras with their Ethiopian smiles, dancing a kind of sinister cancan on the ruins. The only images left are voluptuous feminine ones.—Down below large bas-reliefs running the entire length of the first gallery and showing battle scenes and mythological subjects. One of these is the "churning of the ocean of milk," based on the *Ramayana* (?). All the gods are to be seen here confronting one another in an endless line, towered over at intervals by the greater gods, Brahma, Shiva, the monkey Hanuman, etc., in a sort of giant tug-of-war in which they cling to the body of the snake (Cambodia's national animal, having a seven-headed hood in front of which is carved the parrot-headed garuda). Below this the world of water and mud, of grubs, fish, turtles and crocodiles; up above, the infinite numbers of apsaras dancing around, floating skywards like mosquitoes, like air bubbles.—The afternoon spent alone at the top of this accursed temple, still only dimly aware of a strange feeling of oppression and disgust. In the distance the immense lines of the virgin forest, dull rumbling thunder, the cries of monkeys chasing one another (the apsaras), bonzes in yellow wandering around chanting; one of them behind me with a large knife. —Next day Angkor Thom, the Leper King. Incredible sight of monkeys jumping, chasing one another over the springy ceiling of the forest. Becoming weightless with the momen-

tum of each leap. A life of elasticity and upward thrust. How can our dancers compare?

Paul Claudel
Journal, book IV, October 1921

21 [February], the Prince and some of the mission left for Angkor.

The journalist Tudesq, who died at Saigon, revealed a few hours before his death that four years ago Commaille, Maurice Long, Lord Northcliffe and he had entered one of Angkor's temples despite a warning from the temple guard. This man told them they would all be dead in four years, and he was right. Angkor is one of the most accursed, the most evil, places that I know. I came back ill, and the account I had written of my journey was destroyed in a fire.

Paul Claudel
Journal, book V, February 1925

How to Take a Stone Sculpture

"Let's talk money instead."

"Simple enough! A small bas-relief, almost any statue, will fetch 30,000 francs or so."

"Gold francs?"

"That's asking too much, I'm afraid," Claude smiled.

"A pity! Then I'll want ten at least, and ten more for you; twenty, all told."

"Twenty sculptures."

"A tall order—but feasible, I think."

"And don't forget that a single bas-relief, if it's first-class, a dancing-girl for instance, sells for a couple of hundred thousand francs at least."

"How many stones would go to make it?"

"Three or four."

"And you're sure of selling them?"

"Dead sure. I know the biggest

dealers in London and Paris. And it's easy to fix up a public sale."

"Easy perhaps, but a longish job, eh?"

"There's nothing to prevent your selling directly," Claude explained, "without a public auction, I mean. Pieces of that sort are extremely rare; the boom in far-eastern curios started at the end of the War, and there've been no new finds."

"There's another point; suppose we find the temples—"*We*," Claude murmured to himself—how do you propose to dismantle the stones?"

"That's the problem. I thought of…"

"They're big blocks, if I remember rightly."

"Yes; but don't forget that the Khmer temples were built without foundations or cement. Like castles made of dominoes."

"And each of your dominoes is—wait a bit!—a good yard long by eighteen inches deep and wide. Fifteen hundred pounds or so. Nice little things to handle."

"I'd thought of using rip-saws and removing only the carved surface, just a thin slab. Nothing doing. Hack-saws will be quicker; I've brought some with me. And then we can reckon on the work of time; it has dismantled them pretty effectively; so have the peepuls sprouting in the crannies, not to mention the Siamese fire-raisers who took a hand at the good work, and did it thoroughly."

"I've come across more mounds of broken debris than temples. Don't forget the treasure-hunters, too, have been that way. Till now I've looked on the temples from that angle, myself, more or less."…

The guide's lips were smiling; his forefinger still pointed to the gate.

Never had Claude wanted so urgently to use his fists on a man's face. Clenching his hands, he turned to Perken—to find him smiling, too. Claude's friendship for his comrade turned suddenly to hate. Nevertheless, seeing them all staring at the same point, he followed the direction of their eyes. The main entrance had evidently been a large one and it began, not where he had expected, but on the far side of the wall. What all his companions, familiar with the forest, were looking at was one abutment of it, which stood up from the debris like a pyramid, on the apex of which was a sandstone figure, fragile but intact, crowned with a very delicately wrought diadem. And now he saw, across the leafage, a bird of stone, with a parrot's beak and wings outspread; a slanting sun-beam splintered on its claws. All his anger vanished in that brief but splendid moment. Delight possessed him; he was filled with aimless gratitude, with elation quickly yielding to a maudlin readiness to weep. Aware only of the sculpture, he moved blindly forwards till he stood just in front of the gate. The lintel had fallen, bringing down all that was above it; branches festooned the standing uprights, forming a limp but massive archway, impervious to the sun. Beyond some heaps of fallen stones whose angles stood out black against the light and all but blocked the passage, a thin veil of flimsy wall-plants and slender sprays that ramified in veins of sap was stretched across the tunnel. Perken slashed through it, bringing into view a confused splendour, a haze of broken lights faceted by spiky aloe-leaves. Claude made his way along the passage from stone to stone, steadying

The reconstructed temple of Banteay Srei.

himself against the sides; now and again he rubbed his palms against his trousers to remove the spongy feeling the moss had given them. Suddenly he recalled the ant-infested wall. There, too, a gulf of brightness mottled with leafage had seemed to merge into an opalescent glare, the universal majesty of light brooding above its kingdom of decay.

Before him lay a chaos of fallen stones, some lying flat, but most of them upended; it looked like a mason's yard invaded by the jungle. Here were lengths of wall in slabs of purple sandstone, some carved and others plain, all plumed with pendant ferns. Some bore a red patina, the aftermath of fire. Facing him he saw some bas-reliefs of the best period, marked by Indian influences—he was now close up to them—but very beautiful work; they were grouped round an old shrine, half hidden behind a breastwork of fallen stones. It cost him an effort to take his eyes off them. Beyond the bas-reliefs were the remains of three towers razed to within six feet of the ground. Their mutilated stumps stuck out of such an overwhelming mass of rubble that all the vegetation round them was stunted; they seemed socketed in the debris like candles in their sticks. The shadows had shortened; an unseen sun was climbing up the sky....

Meanwhile Claude had been having the ground cleared of stones, so that the bas-relief should run no risk of being chipped when it fell. While the men were moving away the fallen blocks he examined the figures more attentively. A very light grey-blue moss, like the bloom on European peaches, covered

Sculpture of Shiva and Parvati from Banteay Srei.

one head, which, as was usual in Khmer statues, had smiling lips. Three men put their shoulders to the stone and pushed together. It overbalanced, fell edgewise, and sank into the earth deep enough not to roll over again. In being moved it had made two grooves in the stone on which it rested and along them two armies of dull-hued ants, intent on salvaging their eggs, were hurrying in Indian file. But the second stone, the top of which was now in view, had not been laid in the same way as the first. It was wedged into the main wall between two blocks, each of which weighed several tons. It looked as if, to get it out, the whole wall would need to be demolished, and that was obviously out of the question. If the stones faced with sculpture could only be handled with much difficulty, the other enormous blocks defied human powers. They must be left intact until the passing centuries or peepul-trees sprouting in the ruins should lay them low.

How, he wondered, had the Siamese been able to wreck so many temples? There were tales of elephants harnessed in teams to the walls.... But he had no elephants. The only thing to do was to cut or break the stone so as to detach the sculptured face, whence the last ants were now retreating, from the part embedded in the wall.

Leaning on their improvised levers, the drivers waited. Perken produced his hammer and a chisel. The best way to set about splitting the stone was probably to chisel out a narrow groove in it. He began hammering. But, either because he handled the chisel inexpertly or because the sandstone was too hard, he only succeeded in chipping out the tiniest splinters.... And the natives

A *devata* at Banteay Srei.

impassive, self-willed as a living creature, able to say "No." A rush of blind rage swept over Claude and, planting his feet firmly on the ground, he lunged against the block with all his might. In his exasperation he looked round for some object on which to vent his anger. Perken watched him, his hammer poised in mid-air, with parted lips. Yes, Perken might know the jungle well, but all his forest-lore was useless here; these stones were a sealed book to him. Ah, had he only worked as a mason for six months! He wondered what to do. Should he get the men to pull on it, all together, with a rope? As well scratch it with his nails! And how could one get a rope round it? Yet, he felt, his life hung in the balance, in peril—yes, his very life. So all his obstinacy, his tense determination, the passionate endeavour which had urged him through the jungle had served no other end than this—to bring him up against this obstacle, an immovable stone planted between himself and Siam!…

He breathed again, a slow, deep breath. Claude, too, had a feeling of vast relief. Had he been weaker he would have wept. The world flowed back into him as into a man who has just escaped from drowning. The insensate gratitude he had felt on seeing the first sculptured figure welled up in him anew. Thanks to the fallen stone, he was suddenly in harmony with the forest and the temple. He pictured the three stones as they had been, one above the other; the two dancing-girls were some of the purest work he had ever seen. Well, the next thing was to load them on to the carts.…

André Malraux
The Royal Way, 1935

would, no doubt, be clumsier still.

Claude could not stop staring at the stone. Against the background of trembling leaves and flecks of sunlight, it seemed immensely solid, sure of itself, instinct with ponderous malevolence. The grooves, the stone-dust flickered before his eyes. The last of the ants had vanished, without forgetting a single pulpy egg. Only the stone remained,

Cosmic Symbolism

Scottish photographer John Thomson first drew attention to the symbolic aspect of Khmer architecture. The complex system, further explained by George Coedès and Paul Mus, can best be understood with the help of aerial photographs.

Angkor Wat, the Cosmic Mountain

The building...rises in three terraces, one above the other, and it is out of the highest of the three that the great central tower springs up; four lower or inferior towers rise around it, and the whole structure is probably meant to symbolise Mount Meru, or the centre of the Buddhist universe. This is all the more apparent when we consider that Meru is surrounded by seven circles of rocks; that there are seven circles on the central tower; that the sacred mount is supported on three platforms (corresponding to the three terraces) one platform or layer of earth, one of water, and one of wind; and that it rises out of the ocean. This part of the symbolism is indicated by the temple being surrounded with a moat, and indeed during the rains, when the plain is flooded, the whole stupendous structure would rise (like Meru from the ocean) out of an unbroken sheet of water.

John Thomson
The Straits of Malacca, Indo-China and China, 1875

The Walls and Gates of Angkor Thom

Having shown how the temple-mountain at the center of the royal city is a "representation on a human scale of the mountain which is the axis of the world," George Coedès goes on to discuss the interpretation of the wall and the moat surrounding the city.

The two other essential elements, the ocean, and the wall of rock encircling

Powder compact decorated with a view of Angkor Wat, c. 1960.

the universe, are represented by the moat and the enclosing wall. A Sanskrit poem begins, "The city is enclosed in immense walls like the mountains that girdle the great world. There, contemplating the mounting gold and silver terraces, the inhabitants have no need to wish they could see the peaks of Meru and Kailasa."

This tradition was still so much alive at the time when Angkor was restored by Jayavarman VII that the inscriptions he had placed at the four corners of the city compare the wall to the chain of mountains enclosing the universe, and the surrounding moat to the ocean. "The first pierced the brilliant sky with its pinnacle, the other reached down to the unplumbed depths of the world of serpents. This mountain of victory and this ocean of victory built

by the king, simulated the arc of his great glory."…

In Hindu cosmology the bridge between men and the gods is represented by a rainbow. Paul Mus proved, by finding several corroborating clues, that the bridge with *naga* balustrades which formed a passage over the moat from the world of men to the royal city was an image of the rainbow.…

At Angkor Thom as at Prah Khan and at Banteay Chmar, the bridge with *naga* balustrades…is enhanced by various elements which emphasize its symbol as a rainbow and add a second symbolism even more curious than the first. These bridges lead to the gates of the city which reproduce, at the four cardinal points in a reduced form, the aspect of the temple itself. They represent the extension and

Part of the great bas-relief of the Churning of the Ocean of Milk in the eastern gallery of Angkor Wat.

Phnom Bakheng, the temple at the center of the original city of Yashodharapura.

projection of the royal power emanating from the temple in the four cardinal directions….

But there is more. The long rows of gods and giants holding the *nagas* are not just a whim of the sculptor. They are certainly meant to recall the myth of the churning of the sea, having the three necessary elements for this operation: the ocean represented by the moat of the city, the pivoting mountain represented by the tower over the gate, and the *naga* balustrade representing the cosmic serpent with which the gods pivoted the mountain, as if with a rope, in order to extract the liquid of immortality. The sculptors could be sure that by adding the double row of gods and giants to the combination of the moat-gate-*naga*, the myth of the churning of the sea of milk would be clearly indicated.

By creating the symbol of the churning at the gates of his capital, King Jayavarman VII further established its divinity. In addition a much repeated literary theme, commonly used by the court poets, compared the churning to a great battle from which the king extracted good fortune and victory. From this accumulation of symbolism it is easy to see that the churning of the sea by the pivoting mountain represented a magic operation which assured the nation of victory and prosperity.

George Coedès
Angkor. An Introduction, 1963

Above: Angkor Thom and Angkor Wat. Pages 162–3: The Bayon. Pages 164–5: Angkor Wat. Pages 166–7: Pre Rup.

AIR EN INDOCHINE
5e ESCADRILLE
RUINES D'ANGKOR (CAMBODGE)
LE BAYON
17.11.36

Chronology

Through the joint efforts of art historians, epigraphists, and archaeologists, the chronology of the different periods at Angkor has now been established.

T he beginning of Angkor art: Sandstone sculpture of Vishnu from Rup Arak, Kulen style, first half of the 9th century.

Khmer Art

The oldest known inscriptions, from the south of the region, appear to date back to the third quarter of the 5th century or the beginning of the 6th. They record the existence of buildings that have disappeared and, in at least one case (Neak Ta Dambang Dek), the erection of idols. The earliest surviving images seem to date back no further than the 6th-century reign of Rudravarman, the last attested king of Funan (see Pierre Dupont's work), while no surviving building seems earlier than the beginning of the 7th century, in other words, the Chenla period. The history of Angkor's architecture and statuary, from their earliest appearance at least to the end of the Angkorian period, can be established by studying their evolution (see the work of Philippe Stern) and by referring to inscriptions dated by epigraphists.

Styles of Pre-Angkorian and Angkorian Art

There appear to have been buildings constructed of durable materials in the culture of Oc Eo, capital of Funan, and some brick substructures at Angkor Borei may be contemporary with the earliest inscriptions, but architecture begins to be datable with any degree of certainty only in the 7th century.

The work of Philippe Stern, and later of Gilberte de Coral-Rémusat, Pierre Dupont, and Jean Boisselier, has led to the division of pre-Angkorian and Angkorian art into a series of styles. Each is named after a characteristic monument; the dates, which can be applied to sculpture, have been gradually refined by recourse to epigraphy and comparative studies. The labels denote not watertight categories but fairly loose divisions, within which a style is at its most characteristic only when fully mature. The proposed dates rarely correspond to individual reigns. Almost all are more or less approximate, and there is inevitably a degree of overlap between one style and the next.

Pre-Angkorian period
Phnom Da style (known only from statuary), c. 540(?)–600
Sambor Prei Kuk style, after 600–c. 650
Prei Kmeng style, c. 635–c. 700
Kompong Preah style, c. 706–after 800(?)

Transitional
Kulen style, c. 825–c. 875

Angkorian period
Preah Ko style, c. 875–after 893
Bakheng style, after 893–c. 925
Koh Ker style, 921–c. 945
Pre Rup style (transitional), 947–c. 965
Banteay Srei style, 967–c. 1000
Khleang style, c. 965–c. 1010
Baphuon style, c. 1010–c. 1080 *et seq.*
Angkor Wat style, c. 1100–c. 1175
Bayon style, after 1177–c. 1230

End of the Angkorian Period and Post-Angkorian Period
No specific styles have yet been identified between the end of the Bayon style and the end of the Angkorian period (c. 1431) or in the post-Angkorian period, and the efforts of researchers are complicated by the fact that almost no traditional architectural decoration survives.

The idea that the Bayon style was

The final flowering of Angkor art: Buddha from the Great Preah Khan, Bayon style, late 12th century.

followed by a break with traditional styles and a fairly rapid decline is based primarily on the apparently rather sudden change from an architecture in durable materials to one in light or mixed materials. However, on the evidence of statuary, whose continuous development is better established, this decline appears to have been a much slower process than was at first thought. In architecture, the shift from durable building materials can probably be explained by two major factors: on the one hand, it is clear that the sandstone quarries were virtually exhausted at the end of Jayavarman VII's reign and could no longer supply large-scale building projects; on the other, construction in light or mixed materials was better adapted to the needs of Theravada Buddhism (calling for vast halls that would have been impossible to cover with traditional vaults). The only traces of this architecture in mixed materials are foundations, which are well built but lack distinctive mouldings from which an evolutionary pattern might be discerned (Henri Marchal, "Terrasses Bouddhiques d'Angkor Thom").

Despite this and despite the fact that under Ayuthaya's brief occupation of Angkor after 1431 Thai styles seem to have enjoyed a fleeting popularity in the former capital, at least in statuary, Khmer traditions retained all their vitality in the new centers (Srei Santhor). The renaissance that occurred under Ang Chan with the temporary reoccupation of Angkor in the second half of the 16th century demonstrated that the great traditions were not entirely lost. The restorations and improvements carried out on various monuments (Mnt. 486, Wat Nokor) show genuine continuity in both construction and architectural decoration, while sculpture, although decadent, shows continuing evolution in its ornament and placing.

Jean Boisselier,
Le Cambodge (*Manuel d'Archéologie
d'Extrême-Orient*), 1966

The Occupation of Angkor

The "official" installation of the Khmer monarchy in Angkor is traditionally dated to AD 802, when King Jayavarman II (802–c. 835) proclaimed himself "universal monarch" on Phnom Kulen, a mountain northeast of Angkor, which was the principal source of the region's water. A number of monuments point to an earlier occupation of the area—the temple-mountain of Ak Yom, for example, which Georges Trouvé found buried in the Western Baray dyke. Jayavarman II and his immediate successors built on Phnom Kulen and also in the region of Roluos (southeast of Angkor), where Indravarman I

(877–c. 889) created the temple of Preah Ko, the Bakong pyramid and the Lolei Baray.

We owe the temple of Lolei (located in the center of the *baray* of the same name) to Yashovarman I (889–c. 910), but, more importantly, it was Yashovarman who established his capital on the site of Angkor, calling it Yashodharapura after himself. The city was enclosed by a huge embankment (the remains of which were identified by Victor Goloubew) and surrounded Phnom Bakheng, on the top of which the king constructed his temple-mountain. Yashovarman was also responsible for the Eastern Baray and the temples of Phnom Krom (at the mouth of the Siem Reap River) and Phnom Bok (between Phnom Kulen and Angkor). His immediate successors built the pyramid of Baksei Chamkrong and the temple of Prasat Kravan (restored by Bernard-Philippe Groslier), but Jayavarman IV (928–42) moved his capital to Koh Ker, about fifty miles northeast of Angkor.

The reign of Rajendravarman I (944–c. 967) marked the beginning of major new building works at Angkor: the temples of the Eastern Mebon (in the centre of the Eastern Baray) and Bat Chum, the temple-mountain of Pre Rup, and the Sras Srang lake. Banteay Srei was built by Jayavarman V (968–1000), as was the temple-mountain of Ta Keo (never finished). Suryavarman I (c. 1002–49) built the royal palace enclosure (and, within it, the temple-mountain of Phimeanakas) and was almost certainly responsible for the Western Baray. In the center of the latter Udayadityavarman II (1050–66), to whom we owe the temple-mountain of the Baphuon, built the Western

Mebon and installed in it the bronze statue of Vishnu that Chou Ta-kuan wrongly described as being in the middle of the Eastern Baray.

Suryavarman II (1113–1150?) began a series of building projects that were to continue right up to the sack of Angkor in 1177. They included Angkor Wat, his temple-mountain, the temples of Thommanon, Chau Say Tevoda, and Banteay Samre in Angkor, and, outside Angkor, the temple of Beng Mealea, the central group of the Preah Khan of Kompong Svay, and the temples which line the road from Angkor to Kompong Svay.

Under Jayavarman VII (1181–1218?) the capital underwent major reconstruction. For the first time there was a stone encircling wall, that of Angkor Thom; a temple-mountain of an unprecedented type, the Bayon, was built inside it; new temples were erected, notably Ta Prohm, Preah Khan, Banteay Kdei and Neak Pean; and Jayavarman was also responsible for the Angkor Thom moats and the Preah Khan Baray, as well as for important building works outside the region. These major projects were Angkor's last. After Jayavarman's death only routine building work was undertaken in the city and stone was reserved for the substructures of Buddhist temples, which were otherwise built in light materials.

Bruno Dagens

Suryavarman II holding court, shown in a bas-relief of the southern gallery at Angkor Wat, the temple that he built.

Restoration and Anastylosis

At Angkor Wat there is a c. 1579 inscription that reads, "The king restored the enclosing walls, stone by stone, and rebuilt the roof with its nine-pointed spire."

A Historic or a Living Monument?

The Cambodian kings responsible for restoring Angkor Wat in the 16th century readily referred to the distant predecessor of theirs who had built the temple. Their primary concern, however, was with Angkor Wat as a living shrine rather than as a monument of historic importance, and it seems probable that the few building projects that followed theirs, particularly those instigated by the king of Thailand, were undertaken in the same spirit.

Matters changed when, in 1907, Europe began playing an active role at Angkor. One of the first operations at Angkor Wat was to open up the cella in the central tower, whose doors had been walled in with massive Buddhist sculptures. The object was to restore the building to its "original" state before its adaptation to the country's new religion, Theravada Buddhism. While it was impossible to remove all traces of the monument's active religious life, efforts were henceforth made to confine it to the gallery of the Thousand Buddhas.

The three main shrine-towers at Banteay Srei.

Angkor's other monuments had lost much of their religious significance by the beginning of the 20th century. Later additions, some of them quite extensive, were more or less abandoned—for example, the giant recumbent Buddha set against the Baphuon's western facade, or the equally large sitting Buddha covering Phnom Bakheng's entire eastern facade.

History versus Mystery

In the case of these latter monuments the European approach could be freely adopted and the "original" structure cleared of all accretions, both organic and architectural. It was an approach not universally approved, however. Many of Angkor's visitors, while finding it natural that one should want to remove from the ruins any additions made by ignorant "natives," looked very unfavorably on any attempts to clear those same ruins of the vegetation that gave them their mystery and hence their interest.

The authorities were quick to reach a consensus that satisfied both the romantic hankering for mystery and the opposing interests of those who wanted to rediscover Angkor as it once was. The majority of monuments would be cleared "scientifically," but where ruins and vegetation had produced a particularly felicitous union—Ta Prohm, Ta Som, Neak Pean, for example—they would be left untouched; the Angkor jungle, moreover, would be designated a conservation area.

The Danger of Respecting Old Stones

The program was beset with problems from the start. The trees protected the ruins from the heavy rains, and their roots, while dislocating the walls, also held them together. Once cut down, moreover, they were rapidly replaced by secondary growth of a much more insidious and invasive nature, which ended up smothering what had previously been visible under the foliage. Such work, therefore, often had the effect of eroding the ruins still further and intensifying damage that had previously been limited. There was also no end to it.

The "scientific" response to these problems was timid and ineffectual. After each rainy season maintenance teams endeavored to clean up those sites that had been cleared, but they never had enough workers. In around 1925 chemicals were sprayed in an attempt to kill off the secondary growth, but the process was costly and the results were poor. All other efforts focused on consolidating the ruins as effectively as possible, though—out of respect for their antiquity—any kind of structural tampering was strictly prohibited. Maurice Glaize wrote in 1942: "The directives of those in charge of archaeological efforts in the Indochinese peninsula were…to maintain each monument strictly in the state revealed by the clearing work, and to avoid any alterations to the main structure that were not clearly visible as restoration." There was no question of replacing original elements with new work in the same material, which might be confused with the "real" ruin. On the other hand, numerous sections were missing or irrecoverable. Sandstone is a fragile material and blocks that had fallen to the ground (sometimes shattering in the process) suffered from long contact with the damp earth. Bat droppings also had a highly corrosive effect on the stone.

What was more, since people had continued to live at Angkor, stones from some of the sites had been plundered and recut for use elsewhere.

The little work that was done to reinforce the ruins relied, therefore, exclusively on external supports. Concrete posts shored up overhanging sections of stonework, dislodged when a part of the building had collapsed, and shaky lintels were supported by struts made of concrete or wood. The results were neither attractive nor durable. Sculptures ended up being concealed behind supports and often part of a ruin would collapse leaving a post suspended from a section of wall that it had been designed to reinforce. In the absence of more fundamental consolidation, it was often the tottering ruin which served to support the "restoration" rather than the other way around. The ruins had lost the charm their mantle of foliage had lent them, but the result was neither more solid nor more intelligible to the average viewer.

A Solution: Anastylosis Javanese Style

The relative isolation of those in charge of restoration work at Angkor, and perhaps also the fact that they were having to improvise in an area in which they had not been trained, no doubt explains why until the end of the 1920s no other solutions had been envisaged.

In fact the principle of respecting a ruin as an integral entity was not applied in Europe, where it was widely accepted that a ruined monument could be "re-erected" and the missing components supplied by new work. This type of reconstruction was known as "anastylosis"—literally "re-erection of columns," since in Greek *stylos* signifies "column" and the prefix *ana* conveys the

sense of "re-establishing" or "going back in time." The term was to be used for Cambodia despite the fact that Cambodian architecture rarely uses columns. The theory of anastylosis was expounded by the Greek architect Balanos, whose much-quoted definition runs: "Anastylosis consists in the restoration or re-erection of a monument using its own materials and according to the construction methods proper to it. Anastylosis allows the discreet use, where justified, of new materials to replace missing stones in the absence of which it would be impossible to replace the old components."

The Dutch had been using this technique since the beginning of the century on Indonesian monuments. Borobudur, for example, was restored in this way between 1907 and 1911. By the time Dr. van Stein Callenfels visited Angkor the technique had been perfected, and Henri Marchal described it in detail in his mission report for 1930. The main stages of the restoration process are, in brief, as follows:

1. Cleaning, excavation and plan, search for stones, first attempts at reassembly by laying out on the ground, dismantling of standing sections course by course.

2. Hardening of the ground (with or without a concrete platform), reassembly with insertion of new stones where necessary (these new components are not sculpted, but roughly hewn, and identified by lead markings) and without using mortar for the facing (the stones to be held in place from behind by iron cramps).

Technical Reservations

Marchal was perfectly amenable to the principle of anastylosis, but he had objections to its application at Angkor on purely technical grounds. There was no one at Angkor with the necessary expertise, nor did they have the appropriate equipment, and Marchal foresaw that, as had happened in Java, they would be involved in a lengthy process of trial and error. Moreover, Khmer monuments were more complex than Javanese ones, making it more difficult to find space for the necessary work. More importantly, Angkor's sandstone was softer and more friable than Java's andesite and this, combined with the poor quality of Khmer construction, resulted in much more of it being broken. However, for Marchal "the principal lesson to be learned from the methods applied in Java is the advantage of a more discreet use of cement.... As in Java, the visitor should ideally be unable to see the least trace of cement."

But What About Mystery?

Banteay Srei was unanimously regarded as a success. The restored monument gave an impression of completeness, as the yellow laterite used to supply the missing sections blended in with the yellowish pink of the original sandstone. The temple's magnificent jungle setting was responsible for the rest. Henceforth the technique of anastylosis could be applied at Angkor itself—though not without raising a few protests. Maurice Glaize swept these aside in a lecture he devoted to anastylosis in 1942 after numerous spectacular operations (Neak Pean, Banteay Samre) had enabled him to perfect the technique: "Often...the archaeologist's efforts are met only with mistrust on the part of the 'tourist' who hankers for the picturesque and who, in the midst of the 20th century, travels in style and comfort to visit ruins where he

Reconstruction in progress at Banteay Srei, c. 1930.

One of the last projects supervised by Henri Marchal, at Banteay Srei Damdek, 1952.

expects to experience the exhilaration of a Mouhot discovering Angkor Wat in 1860. This tourist is driven by an outdated individualism, and all that counts for him is a romanticism fueled by spectacular effects, as symbolized by a section of wall crumbling in the passionate tentacled embrace of voracious trees. The Curator of the monuments is no more than the stage-manager of this vegetal orgy" ("L'Anastylose, Méthode de Reconstruction des Monuments Anciens. Son Application à l'Art Khmer," *Cahiers de l'Ecole Française d'Extrême-Orient*, no. 29, Hanoi, 1942).

Glaize sees no point in preserving ruins in "that dilapidated state" that "prevents the seeker from going beyond the emotion he feels as an artist or poet." "True romanticism," he continues, "is the sort of romanticism

that can sow among the old stones of a ruined sanctuary the leaven of something that no longer exists," and he concludes: "[Anastylosis] has, to my mind, the ineluctable character of a solution that perfectly fits the problem. It cannot fail, provided that its motto remains that of any self-respecting archaeologist: time, patience, and reflection."

A New Kind of Anastylosis

Not all Angkor's reconstructions weathered equally well. Many of the ruins were disfigured by patches of cement. Subsidence posed an even more serious problem, since many of the original stones were in a poor condition when they were replaced and unable to support the loads they were being required to bear. Bernard-Philippe Groslier was quick to recognize the limitations of anastylosis, as Jacques

Dumarçay had put it, "without internal reinforcement or protective measures designed at least to counteract any changes in the sandstone." The biggest problem with sandstone was humidity, and the only answer was to isolate the reconstructed building on new cement foundations. Reinforcements, also in cement, concealed behind the facade of the building reduced the load placed on the old stones.

This more fundamental type of anastylosis was profoundly disruptive. The finished effect may have been pleasing to the eye, and the preparatory work may have provided an intimate knowledge of the monument's construction, but the technique was only used as a last resort. As Groslier wrote in 1976, after leaving Angkor, "From the start we determined upon this (restoration) work and devised it for the sole purpose of saving monuments and because it appeared to be the only effective method, though not of course in order to "restore" their appearance, however reasonable an objective that might be in certain cases. Conversely, in many instances where we felt unable to proceed or uncertain as to how to proceed we preferred to avoid any premature action which might have a compromising effect in the future. In a word, this type of restoration is akin to surgery: that is, it should only be applied as a last resort and with the knowledge that it will always leave scars" (*Travaux et Perspectives de l'Ecole Française d'Extrême-Orient en Son 75e Anniversaire*, Paris, 1976).

Bruno Dagens

A new piece of sandstone being cut during restoration work at the Baphuon, 1968.

Tourists in Angkor

In 1925 a visitor named Roland Dorgelès reported, "Arriving from Phnom Penh, one suddenly meets up with a gigantic notice where one is amazed to read: 'Pilgrims to Angkor, Turn Right.'"

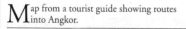

M ap from a tourist guide showing routes into Angkor.

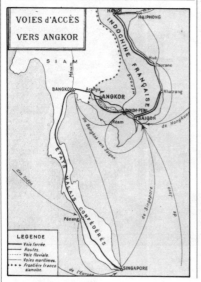

Angkor in the 1920s: Tourist Routes

Most of Angkor's principal monuments were directly connected by road and could be visited with the minimum amount of exertion. From the early 1920s tourists had a choice of two routes—the longer simply being an extension of the shorter.

The Short Route

The short route started at Angkor Wat and went from there to the Bayon, via the foot of Phnom Bakheng (at which point it was traditional to mount an elephant) and through the southern gate, some of whose giants had been among the first of Angkor's monuments to be re-erected. From the Bayon visitors proceeded to the royal square and the Terrace of the Leper King— which no tourist was allowed to miss. After that they headed east; beyond the Victory Gate they would have caught a glimpse of Thommanon and Chau Say Tevoda flanking the road, among the trees. Crossing the river, they continued to Ta Keo, a wonderful geometric complex with minimal decoration.

The road then ran alongside Ta Prohm, which, thanks to a decision taken at around this time, had been deliberately left in its ruined state, festooned with vegetation. Branching off from the main track here and heading into the jungle, tourists could experience for themselves some of what earlier visitors to Angkor had felt—Mouhot, for example, or Paul Claudel, who wrote in his journal in 1921: "Ta Prohm buried under vegetation and trees. An atmosphere of fever and decay." Next came Banteay Kdei and finally, a refreshing sight, the great Sras Srang lake.

The road back to Angkor Wat cut through the jungle, offering a glimpse of

One of the towers of Ta Prohm, photographed by Lucien Fournereau during his visit to Angkor in 1887–8.

the ruined brick towers of Prasat Kravan. It ended in front of the temple moats, which even then were beginning to be invaded by water hyacinth, the nightmare of all Angkor's curators.

The Long Route

This followed the short route to the royal square and then led straight to the northern gate, before angling off to run alongside Preah Khan, with its causeways (like Angkor Thom's) bordered by giants leading up to the gates. The road then led east, passing over the northern dyke of Chou Ta-kuan's "Northern Lake," the Preah Khan Baray. It was dried up and overgrown, but at its center the glorious island (Neak Pean) was still much as it had been. A giant banyan still encompassed the central tower rising in the center of a small circular lake, whose water flowed out through gargoyles towards successive lakes. Louis Finot and Victor Goloubew had recently identified it as a representation of Lake Anavatapta, the source, in Buddhist tradition, of the four great rivers that water the universe.

At the eastern extremity of the "lake" was Ta Som, its face-tower (which served as a gate) also embedded in a banyan, probably the most photographed banyan in the world. Then, bearing south, the road entered another dried-up artificial lake, this one larger still, the Eastern Baray, passing close to the central island, the Eastern Mebon, an enormous laterite mound crowned with five brick towers. Then, just before Sras Srang, where the long route rejoined the shorter, came Pre Rup with its five brick towers, still partially decorated with stucco.

The program took four and a half days. If there was any time left visitors could continue as far as Roluos to see the pre-Angkorian temples there, or head west from Angkor Thom in the direction of the Western Baray. Beng Mealea and the Great Preah Khan, far to the east, tended to be the preserve of foresters and hunters.

Bruno Dagens

The ruins of Phimeanakas, photographed by Lucien Fournereau in 1887–8.

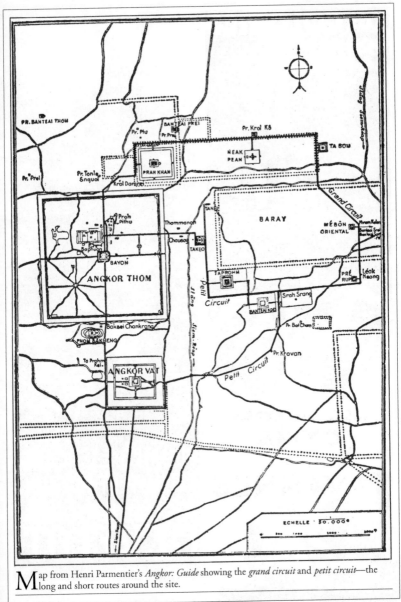

Map from Henri Parmentier's *Angkor: Guide* showing the *grand circuit* and *petit circuit*—the long and short routes around the site.

The French colonial expositions of 1922 and 1931 involved reconstructions of Angkor (above, at Marseilles in 1922), and its enthusiastic use in the promotion of such products as watches, gun cartridges, refrigerators, and clothing.

Further Reading

Audric, John, *Angkor and the Khmer Empire*, R. Hale, London, 1972

Aymonier, Etienne, *Le Cambodge* (*Manuel d'Archéologie d'Extrême-Orient*), E. Leroux, Paris, 1901–3

Boisselier, Jean, *Le Cambodge*, 1966, Paris

———, *Trends in Khmer Art*, 1989

Bouillevaux, Charles-Emile, *Voyage dans l'Indo-Chine 1848–1856*, 1858

———, *L'Annam et le Cambodge—Voyages et Notices Historiques*, Paris, 1874

Boulbet, Jean, and Bruno Dagens, "Les Sites Archéologiques de la Région du Bhnam Gulen," *Arts Asiatiques*, 27, 1973

Briggs, Lawrence, *The Ancient Khmer Empire*, American Philosophical Society, Philadelphia, 1951

———, *A Pilgrimage to Angkor, Ancient Khmer City*, Holmes, Oakland, California, 1943

Carpeaux, Charles, *Les Ruines d'Angkor, de Duong-Duong, et de My-Son*, 1908

Chou Ta-kuan: see Pelliot

Coedès, George, *Angkor: An Introduction*, trans. Emily Floyd Gardiner, Oxford University Press, New York, 1963

Cohen, Joan Lebold, *Angkor: Monuments of the God-Kings*, Harry N. Abrams, New York, 1973

Coral-Rémusat, Gilberte de, *L'Art Khmer: les Grandes Etapes de son Evolution*, Editions d'Art et d'Histoire, Paris, 1940

Delaporte, Louis, *Les Monuments du Cambodge*, 1914–24

———, *Voyage au Cambodge, l'Architecture Khmère*, C. Delagrave, Paris, 1880

Fergusson, James, *A History of Indian and Eastern Architecture*, 1876

Finot, Louis, Victor Goulobew, and George Coedès, *Le Temple d'Angkor Vat*, Van Oest, Paris, 1927–32

Fournereau, Lucien, *Les Ruines Khmères*, 1891

———, and J. Porcher, *Les Ruines d'Angkor, Etude Artistique et Historique*, 1890

Freeman, Michael, *Angkor: The Hidden Glories*, Houghton Mifflin, Boston, 1990

Giteau, Madeleine, *The Civilization of Angkor*, trans. Katherine Watson, Rizzoli, New York, 1976

———, *Khmer Sculpture and the Angkor Civilization*, Harry N. Abrams, New York, 1966

Glaize, Maurice, *Les Monuments du Groupe d'Angkor*, A. Maisonneuve, Paris, 1963

Groslier, Bernard-Philippe, *Angkor: Art and Civilization*, trans. E. E. Smith, Praeger, New York, 1966

Groslier, Bernard-Philippe, *Angkor et le Cambodge au XVIe Siècle d'après les Sources Portugaises et Espagnoles*, Presses Universitaires de France, Paris, 1958

Groslier, George, *Recherches sur les Cambodgiens*, A. Challamel, Paris, 1921

Jacques, Claude, *Angkor*, Borbas, Paris, 1990

Lee, Sherman, *Ancient Cambodian Sculpture*, Asia Society, New York, 1969

Loti, Pierre, *Un Pèlerin d'Angkor*, Calmann-Lévy, Paris, 1912

Lunet de Lajonquière, Etienne-Edmond, *Inventaire Déscriptif des Monuments du Cambodge*, 1902–11

Macdonald, Malcolm, *Angkor*, Cape, London, 1958

Malraux, André, *The Royal Way*, trans. Stuart Gilbert, 1935

Marchal, Henri, *Les Temples d'Angkor*, A. Guillot, Paris, 1955

Mouhot, Henri, *Travels in the Central Parts of Indo-China (Siam), Cambodia and Laos*, 1864

Parmentier, Henri, *L'Art Khmer Classique*, Editions d'Art et d'Histoire, Paris, 1939

Pelliot, Paul, *Mémoires sur les Coutumes de Cambodge de Tcheou Ta-kouan*, A. Maisonneuve, Paris, 1951

Pym, Christopher, *The Ancient Civilization of Angkor*, Mentor, New York, 1968

———, *Henri Mouhot's Diary*, Oxford University Press, New York, 1966

Riboud, Marc, *Angkor: The Serenity of Buddhism*, Thames and Hudson, London, 1993

Stern, Philippe, *Les Monuments Khmers du Style du Bayon et Jayavarman VII*, Presses Universitaires, Paris, 1965

Thomson, John, *Antiquities of Cambodia*, 1867

———, *The Straits of Malacca, Indo-China, and China*, 1875, repr. 1993

Villemereuil, A. de, ed., *Explorations et Missions de Doudart de Lagrée, Extraits de Ses Manuscrits*, 1883

List of Illustrations

Index

Acknowledgments

The author wishes to thank Jean Boulbet, Jacques Dumarçay, Claude Jacques, Pierre Pichard, and Sylvie Watelet, as well as Bernadette Grandcolas, Jean-Paul and Monique Schneider, Françoise, Nicolas, and Catherine. The publishers wish to thank Madame François Dellesmillières, Pierre Dumonteil, Mrs. Judy Godfrey, Jérôme Hayaux du Tilly, Banque Indosuez, Annie Jacques, Caroline Mathieu, Pierre Pitrou, Christiane Rageau, Gérard Turpin, and Lyne Thornton for their invaluable help.

Photograph Credits

Text Credits

Grateful acknowledgment is made for use of material from the following: George Coèdes, *Angkor: An Introduction*, translated by E. F. Gardiner, Oxford University Press, Hong Kong and New York (pp. 158–160) and André Malraux, *The Royal Way*, translated by Stuart Gilbert, Methuen & Co., London, and Random House, New York (pp. 153–7)

Bruno Dagens was born in the Netherlands and brought up in North Africa and Strasbourg, France. A former member of the Ecole Française d'Extrême-Orient, he was introduced to archaeology by Daniel Schlumberger in Afghanistan. In 1965 he went to Cambodia and worked for the Angkor Conservation Service for seven years, studying temple iconography, organizing and restoring the sculptures in the depot at Angkor, and investigating the region's mineral deposits. He also translated a Sanskrit treatise on architecture, drawing on his knowledge of the Angkor temples. After a period teaching at Louvain, Belgium, he spent nine years in Pondicherry in southern India studying Shaivite texts and a group of temples located on the site of a future dam. In 1985 and 1994 he returned briefly to Angkor. Dagens is currently teaching at the University of Paris–III, carrying out research in Thailand, and coordinating on behalf of UNESCO a project to conserve the Wat Phu temple in Laos.

To Cathy and Nicolas
in memory of their friends at Phum Trean

Translated from the French by Ruth Sharman

Editor: Sharon AvRutick
Typographic Designer: Elissa Ichiyasu
Design Supervisor: Miko McGinty
Assistant Designer: Tina Thompson
Text Permissions: Neil Ryder Hoos

Library of Congress Catalog Card Number: 94–77943

ISBN 0–8109–2801–9

Copyright © 1989 Gallimard

English translation copyright © 1995 Harry N. Abrams, Inc., New York, and Thames and Hudson Ltd., London

Published in 1995 by Harry N. Abrams, Inc., New York
A Times Mirror Company

Printed and bound in Italy by Editoriale Libraria, Trieste